Anyone can be an

Expert Skier

Harald R. Harb

Anyone Can Be An Expert Skier 1–The New Way to Ski
A Getfitnow.com Book

Hatherleigh Press/Getfitnow.com Books
An Affiliate of W.W. Norton and Company, Inc.
5-22 46th Avenue, Suite 200
Long Island City, NY 11101
Toll Free 1-800-528-2550
Visit our websites getfitnow.com and hatherleighpress.com

Disclaimer:
Before beginning any exercise and recreational skiing program, consult your physician. The author and the publisher disclaim any liability, personal or professional, resulting from the application or misapplication of any of the information in this publication. Skiing is an inherently dangerous sport. You should not depend solely on information gleaned from this book or any other for your skiing safety. This is not a substitute for personal instruction in skiing. Your use of this book indicates your assumption of the risk of skiing and is an acknowledgement of your own sole responsibility for your skiing safety.

Anyone Can Be An Expert Skier books are available for bulk purchase, special promotions and premiums. For more information on reselling and special purchase opportunities, please call us at 1-800-528-2550 and ask for the Special Sales Manager.

LIBRARY OF CONGRESS CATALOGING AND PUBLICATION DATA UPON REQUEST
ISBN: 1-57826-177-5

Interior Layout and Design, Photomontages, and Illustrations by Diana Rogers

Cover Design by Peter Gunther

Text Photos by Grafton Smith, except
Burnham Arndt: pp.175,184,185,189,190
Byron Hetzler: Chapters 9 & 11; pp. 32,33,97,146,147,159,174,204,205
Darren Jacklin: Chapter 2: pp. 42,43,44,52,53,63,81,84,85,96,101,104,105
Carl Scofield: pp. 182,188

10 9 8 7 6 5 4 3
Printed in Canada on acid-free paper.

Contents

Preface to 2nd Printing

It's been two years since the book and video *Anyone can be an Expert Skier* were published. Since then, Diana Rogers and I have completely devoted ourselves to our company, Harb Ski Systems. One of our corporate missions is to make skiing more fun and easier to learn. This can be accomplished by using a more effective ski instruction method, and by selecting and tailoring proper ski equipment. The PMTS™ Direct Parallel program is gaining recognition as the effective, direct parallel way to learn skiing and to help experienced skiers improve.

Our latest book, the *Primary Movements Teaching System Instructor Manual* was published in late autumn of 1998. It features the complete PMTS™ Direct Parallel program from beginner to expert, as well as sections to improve the teaching ability of ski instructors. In November, 1999, we released the accompanying *PMTS™ Direct Parallel Movements Green/Blue* video that displays the movements of the system up to and including blue levels.

We implemented an instructor accreditation program, to train and evaluate instructors who use the Primary Movements Teaching System. With training in biomechanics, alignment, and teaching technique as well as the Primary Movements Teaching System, the accreditation program surpasses current instructor standards. There are three levels of instructor accreditation: green, blue, and black.

Harb Ski Systems is now offering a special, high-end program for ski instructors and ski shop technicians: the Personal Skiing Consultant certification. We find there is a need for highly qualified individuals to perform skiing consulting services. We also see more and more skiers frustrated with the piecemeal approach to setting up their skiing. Skiers are realizing that matching equipment, alignment, and technique is essential for an unequaled skiing experience. Our ongoing courses provide training, technical understanding and experience for individuals to become a PSC. Personal

Skiing Consultants must attain the black level in the Primary Movements Teaching System accreditation and certification as a Harb Skier Alignment System Technician. Harb Ski Systems is training candidates for this program in the 1999 season.

In December, 1997, we unveiled our website, **www.harbskisystems.com**. Since then we have worked diligently to make it an informative site where skiers can learn about our programs, find accredited Primary Movements Teaching System instructors and licensed ski schools, read our most current information about instruction and alignment, and communicate with us via e-mail.

The second printing of this book allows me to bring you up to date with important changes in the world of skiing. Ski instruction is changing with the growth of independent camps and coaching sessions. "Independent" means outside the controlling influences of traditional teaching organizations. This is a positive development for skiers, offering a choice in technique and teaching approach.

Highly respected professionals accept the Primary Movements Teaching System

We are pleased to have influenced a number of the key independents with our Primary Movements Teaching System. Rob and Eric DesLauriers use the principles of the system as the foundation of movements taught at their Extreme Camps. With this application, they demonstrate the versatility of primary movements for off-piste and all-mountain skiing.

Lito Tejada-Flores uses many principles of the system at his very successful camps located in Aspen. I was honored to be asked to ski in Lito's latest video, *Breakthrough on Skis III*, to demonstrate what he calls "Phantom Edging".

John Clendenin, owner of the Ski & Board Doctors in Aspen, Colorado, is a black-level accredited Primary Movements Teaching System instructor. Through the Ski Doctors he provides Ski Simulator Lessons and "Camps With The Champs". John is a former two-time World Freestyle Champion who offers his highly effective indoor sessions on a ski deck/ski simulator at the Aspen Club and Spa. Skiing with John is a pleasure, on snow and on the deck. I am very impressed with the effectiveness of the deck as a teaching tool. Habits that skiers find difficult to change on snow are changed in a few lessons on the simulator. The environment is perfect for private ski instruction. The benefits of a ski deck lesson are one-on-one contact with the coach, complete safety, instant feedback, and a warm room. The experience is directly transferable to real skiing. John's deck lessons follow a special version of PMTS™ Direct Parallel developed for deck instruction.

Be Aware

I have received feedback and observed that some aspects of the Primary Movements Teaching System are being incorporated into traditional teaching. This was bound to happen, since the primary movements are so effective. Adding parts of the Primary Movements Teaching System to traditional instruction will improve the traditional lesson but won't provide the full benefits of a complete PMTS™ Direct Parallel lesson. Accredited Primary Movements Teaching System instructors are trained extensively to analyze movement and to use primary movements to help skiers progress. Untrained instruction may yield the benefits of the "Phantom Move" but as most of us who have studied the Primary Movements Teaching System understand, that is just one aspect in the development of a repertoire of efficient movements.

The *Primary Movements Teaching System Instructor Manual* includes sections that address biomechanics and physics to create an accurate understanding of skiing. In addition, our instructor accreditation program offers training in equipment performance and alignment recognition. Without this accurate understanding, skiing movements can easily be misinterpreted. Although you may hear increased use of the word "tipping" in ski teaching, it doesn't mean the instructor is trained or accredited in PMTS™ Direct Parallel. The new corporate name for Chrysler is Daimler/Chrysler, and the Chrysler you buy from the merged company may be better than what was previously available, but when you buy a Chrysler, you are not getting a Mercedes. You can find a list of licensed resorts and accredited instructors on our website, www.harbskisystems.com. Ask for an accredited Primary Movements Teaching System instructor to make sure you receive a PMTS™ Direct Parallel lesson.

PMTS™ Direct Parallel Pioneers and Supporters of Harb Ski Systems

In the few years that Harb Ski Systems has been in operation, several individuals have consistently given of their time and energy to support us. Their dedication to our company and our programs has been instrumental in our success thus far.

Mel Brown

What is there to say about Mel that would surprise anyone that knows her? That she is dedicated to excellence, that she wants the best for her guests and instructors, and that she is a loyal, unwavering, positive influence? No, anyone who knows Mel already knows her dedication to these values. In many ways, Mel's encouragement influenced me to start Harb Ski Systems. I trust her extensive business instincts, knowledge, and methods. She has an unbelievably strong grasp of efficient skiing movement. I rank her with the best ski coaches, including those at the international level of skiing. Thankfully, someone recognized her ability, as she became the youngest examiner in the Central Division of PSIA.

Mel operated the most efficient and effective ski school in the industry at Wilmot Mountain, Wisconsin. She is one of our first Primary Movements Teaching System examiners and Wilmot was our first licensed Primary Movements Teaching System ski school. She and her fellow Primary Movements Teaching System examiner in the Central Division, Robert Emery, have conducted very successful training and accreditation sessions. In the face of much opposition and resistance, she perseveres in convincing instructors and examiners that the Primary Movements Teaching System is the skiing system of the future.

Above all, Mel loves to ski and finds enormous pleasure in bringing the sport to others. She dedicates herself to increasing education and skiing enjoyment for everyone she knows.

Robert Emery

Robert is a lifelong skier, educator, and innovator. He is the former President of PSIA's Central Division and a Primary Movements Teaching System trainer and examiner. He is one of the demonstrators in our current video production, *PMTS™ Direct Parallel Movements Green/Blue*. Although Robert is an attorney, a judge, and a law professor, much of his energy and enjoyment is derived from helping other skiers fully develop their skiing potential. He has extraordinary communication skills, cutting the often overly shrouded mystery of skiing technique to the core, where efficient movement and understanding reside.

Fundamentally grounded in the understanding of physics and biomechanics, Robert makes skiing easy, clear and fun. He transcends the commonly perceived image of ski trainers and examiners, communicating easily, openly and directly, in an unselfish manner, with all skiers and instructors.

This introduction of Robert wouldn't be complete without acknowledging his invaluable assistance and counsel to Harb Ski Systems, Diana, and me in our business ventures.

Rich Messer

Rich is one of my oldest friends. We started teaching skiing together for Emo Heinrich at Stratton, Vermont, in 1972. Rich is a former PSIA Eastern Examiner and ski school director. He is a true shaped ski pioneer. He skied on shaped skis and believed they would change the ski industry before many of us knew what they were.

Rich is presently the ski school director at Silver Creek Ski and Golf Ranch, Colorado. He has been a firm believer in the Primary Movements Teaching System from the beginning. Rich is an innovator and meticulous student of skiing technique. He has a highly refined understanding of ski technique and is completely devoted to providing the best ski instruction experience to all of his guests. Rich is one of our first Primary Movements Teaching System trainers and examiners.

Equipment

Boots

This book has a complete description of alignment methods we have found successful for the past four years. Equipment and alignment is closely scrutinized in our efforts to achieve optimal balance for skiers. A boot with aggressive forward lean and fixed, high ramp inclination angles will never allow you to achieve optimal skiing. We have retrofitted many instructors who were having great difficulty with their skiing. Few realized the source of their problem was the design of their boots. Previously accepted boot fitting standards may not satisfy your balancing needs. We provide a complete retail and boot-fitting center at our Harb Skier Alignment Center at Silver Creek, Colorado. Our approaches to achieve optimal balance go well beyond making the inside of the boot feel good. Although comfort is still an important consideration, equally important is selecting the appropriate boot for your alignment. Lateral alignment affects balance in one plane. Fore/aft balance is affected by body proportions and boot ramp and forward lean angles. If the boots you buy don't have adjustments for forward lean or sole ramp inclination you are limited to the position the boot determines for you. A boot with fixed angles can be fine if you have the right proportions. Analyzing the skier's body proportions and boot settings to determine optimal fore/aft balance is a critical part our program. Our work with ski boots has demonstrated that people with different body proportions and leg length benefit from customized and individualized ramp inclination and forward lean angles. This is not just a heel lift! We have developed a Posture Performance Grid to establish recommendations for skiers of all different body proportions.

Skis

Skis continue to evolve. Shaped skis of two years ago rarely match the products available today. The latest trend has been the "mid-fat" skis. I remember doing a ski test four years ago for *Skiing Magazine* in which I recommended the K2 Three model. My skiing contemporaries thought I had gone soft because the K2 Three was an intermediate ski, not a macho performance ski. It turns out the dimensions of the K2 Three are all the rage for today's mid-fat skis. This design trend makes a great deal of sense as its dimensions provide performance that make skis enjoyable. The mid-fat skis are wider under foot, averaging about 67 mm waist width. This width provides stability, flotation, balance and strong edging characteristics. If you want to select one ski for all purposes, the mid-fat ski will do it all. Be careful to distinguish between mid-fat all-purpose skis and extreme skis, also known as freeride skis. Manufacturers are building very stiff, wider skis for the "Extreme Skier", whatever small fraction of the skier population they represent. These skis are not versatile enough for bumps or short turns on groomed. The width dimension guidelines for all-purpose skis are around 105 mm at the tip, 67 mm waist, and 98 mm at the tail. If you select a ski with dimensions close to these, you will have a versatile ski.

Tradition dies hard but the slalom ski has finally succumbed to the shaped ski revolution. The World Cup slalom racing ski, the last bastion of pencil-straight skis, is now a true hourglass shape. They're also short: many of the 200 pound racers use 180 cm or shorter. The women World Cup skiers are on 160 to 170 cm lengths. Now we can go out on our 180 cm skis and never feel inferior again.

Short Shapes

Trick skis with upturned tails, as short as 113 cm, are the rage for the half pipe crowd but have little application for serious skiing. Beginner skis are also shaped, coming from shaped ski origins in lengths anywhere from 113 cm to 145 cm. These are the skis used by PMTS™ Direct Parallel ski schools. We are fortunate that ski schools interested in direct parallel have seen the value in the short shaped skis as a learning tool. The ultimate, direct parallel learning ski for beginners has yet to be developed, but the current products work well. The future looks very bright as development continues with the present generation of skis. I have no doubt that the future of skiing holds great opportunities for fast learning. With further ski development, alignment and PMTS™ Direct Parallel, skiing can become one of the easiest sports to enjoy in a short, two-hour introductory lesson.

Closing Thoughts

In the "Closing Thoughts" chapter of the first printing of this book, I predicted that consolidation of resort ownership and competition between the major resort owners would provide improved services to skiers while potentially making skiing more affordable. Although the basic premises I expressed have developed as I imagined, I need to update where I now see the consolidation trend leading. The competition between corporations that own major ski resorts may have headed in the wrong direction. Although I believe in competition, this game may be detrimental in the long run. It has become obvious to most observers that the ski resort corporations like American Ski Company, Vail Resorts, and Intrawest are real estate developers. The competition no longer revolves around providing better services, skiing, or access. It has become a real estate play for more and bigger condos and houses. Do you find yourself paying for parking - parking that moves further away from the slopes every season? Land that used to be parking lots is now covered with high-rises blocking the view to the slopes. Have you arrived at a ski resort and observed a city skyline like the one you just tried to leave behind?

In the beginning, in an effort to attract skiers who were real estate buyers, the resorts upgraded facilities with new, high-speed lifts, better grooming and snowmaking. What will happen to these facilities and this infrastructure when the real estate is gone? If we consider that no major ski resort is profitable or can survive on lift tickets sales, which resorts will be able to afford maintenance and upgrades of the skiing facility? If it is reasonable to predict that the stock value of these major corporate entities will fall as the real estate play is exhausted, what will these corporations do to maintain shareholder value and increase revenue? Stockholders don't have many options other than to sell before the stock collapses.

American Ski Company expanded so fast, borrowing and buying, that after an average season they had to sell more than a half interest in the company to survive. What happens when a bad season strikes? ASC could not secure development and operation capital other then from issuing junk bonds or selling into a partnership.

The people behind the corporations are real estate raiders, similar to the timber barons in the 19th century. The trend will be to unload the liabilities (resorts) before all the fixed assets are exhausted. Some may be able to get out before the inflated value of their stock crashes. We are in the best economy in history, yet skier visits are dropping. What will happen if there is an economic downturn for a few years - a natural economic occurrence? Is the exuberance of development justified or will we see some ski resorts as the abandoned boomtowns of the twenty-first century? Keep your eye on the development of ski resorts and make sure you are investing because you love to ski and like the area year-round. If you are investing to see a profit from a resale, be aware that the peak may have been reached.

Harald Harb
November, 1999

About the Author

I was born in Schwaz, Austria, in 1949. From an early age, skiing was part of my life as my father was a ski racer, and a certified Austrian and Tirolian Instructor.

Although growing up in Eastern Canada I looked for every opportunity to ski, I always dreamt of racing for the Austrian Ski Team. By today's standards, I started racing late. Except for a few weekend races in Quebec, where I lived, I didn't start seriously training until at seventeen, I moved on my own to Alberta. I skied with the Alberta Ski Team and in my first season placed second in the Canadian National Junior Championships. When I was eighteen I raced in my first World Cup races. From 1969-71 I raced with the Canadian National Ski Team, on the Can-Am circuit and in some World Cup races. In 1973, I was the Overall Pro Champion of the Eastern Regional Circuit.

For the next twenty years I dedicated myself to coaching and directing racing programs. My teaching and technical curiosity came from my drive to produce the best skiing racers on any racecourse. I developed an extensive background in ski coaching as a Program Director and National Ski Team Development Coach. I directed and coached programs that produced several of the USA's most successful National Team Members and Olympic Medalists, including Tommy Moe. I also had the fortune to coach the woman's and men's World Extreme Champions, Kim Reichhelm and Chris Davenport, when they were in their racing development years.

While coaching in Alaska, I tried out for and made the National Demonstration Team. Making the team changed the direction of my career. I started to focus on improving recreational skiers and improving the present teaching system. The existing system never made sense to me, especially after having developed World Cup racers using my own, completely different methods during my coaching career.

I found that the majority of skiers and instructors I trained had two problems that limited their progress. The movements they learned didn't work and their alignment was faulty. I thought of a way to help skiers with alignment: the Alignment Center concept was born. The program took off after just two years, thanks to the coverage I got from Charlie Meyers, of *The Denver Post*, and Craig McNeil, of the *Denver Rocky Mountain News*. Thanks also go to *Snow Country* and *Skiing* magazines for their wonderful support through coverage of my alignment and biomechanical programs. The success of the alignment center approach is based on the fact that it worked for students and instructors alike. It created immediate improvement in people's skiing and that caught the ski industry's attention.

Now I have my own company, Harb Ski Systems, and I continue to be an educator of skiers, training ski schools and ski instructors nationwide. I travel every winter to train and coach skiers and instructors in the Primary Movements Teaching System, and in the Harb Skier Alignment System. I work with numerous skiers in group and private lessons to help them meet their skiing goals. You can find out more about Harb Ski Systems, and how to experience our programs, by visiting our web site for the latest schedules and details: **www.harbskisystems.com**.

Acknowledgements

I first wrote my ideas for Primary Movements five years ago. Although the ideas were just a beginning, they were tested on a handful of skiers and they worked. This book took shape over the years in many forms. This final version would not have been possible without the contributions of these great individuals.

Jerry Muth, my boss and friend at my first job in Colorado, made the materials in this book possible by believing and supporting them. Jerry has always been a champion of his employees. He brings out the best in people by demonstrating hard work, intelligence, and organization. Jerry sets high standards through his leadership, work ethic, and management approach. Jerry made Primary Movements possible by allowing them to be trained and used in a real ski school situation. Jerry also wanted the Performance Center concept to be offered, the first of its kind in the world, to the public, and it worked. Without his unselfish leadership and true vision of skier service, skiers would not be benefiting from these ideas.

Diana Rogers is the true unsung hero of this work. Diana is an aerospace engineer by trade, a graduate of the University of Colorado with a Master's degree from Stanford. She is an accomplished trainer of the Primary Movements Teaching System. Diana's understanding of skiing, skiing mechanics, and human anatomy and ski performance is without equal. Her background in physics and science make her one of the few authorities of ski use and design. She has the communication skills and knowledge that give her the ability to train the trainers of skiing. Her logical methods of presentation have riveted ski instructors to her training from Winter Park to Aspen. Diana has operated and managed a Performance Center, she builds accurate foot beds, and teaches skiers with unbelievable precision. All of this, and she does it with simplicity and modesty. Diana has worked side by side with me on this book. Without her incredible computer skills and hours of assembling the photomontages, this book would not exist. She taught herself how to design and assemble these beautiful layouts in less then a month. She is irreplaceable as a colleague and ski professional.

Kim Peterson provided reason when idealism ruled my energy to revolutionize. He is a calming, sober influence in my often exuberant and emotional dedication to ski instruction and education. Kim is a unique educator and friend who has guided and advised me through more pitfalls than I want to admit or can realize. Kim's educational insight and techniques have the potential to revolutionize the way ski movement is presented. He provides hope that one day the teaching side of ski instruction will be equally valued and understood as the movement side.

John Feig is a ski guru and ski biomechanics pioneer. He is a practicing physiotherapist and foot bed designer. John understands the dynamics of the foot in skiing as few others do. He has helped with US World Cup athletes and, thanks to John, they have produced outstanding results. John is a colleague whom I trust and reference whenever my theories advance beyond my knowledge. He is instrumental in guiding our alignment process.

Robert Hintermeister is a Doctor of Biomechanics and Director of the Steadman Research Foundation in Vail, Colorado. Bob is a doctor of movement understanding and he loves to ski. I couldn't have found a better person with whom to test my understanding and theories. In the past five years he has helped to guide my understanding of muscle activity in skiing as well as to ground my understanding of the resulting dynamics from movement. Few engineers I have met can explain skiing with Bob's clarity and precision.

Bob LaMarche was the editor for *Snow Country* magazine when I began my editorial career. He is now editor of the New York Times Special Events publications. Bob is a close friend who took a risk by trusting that my different approach to skiing would be interesting to readers. He slogged through my early writing attempts and made them comprehensible. Without his support, I might never have written a book.

Thanks to the friends and colleagues who reviewed the book and gave me valuable feedback. Diana and I have incorporated most, if not all, of your suggestions. We wanted to do more and add more ideas, but finally the deadline overruled.

Foreword

This works! Harald Harb's understanding of alpine skiing is articulated in this book as a complete system which is biomechanically founded and which takes into account current ski and boot design, the skier's physical alignment, his or her ankle and foot physiology, and the basic skiing movements used by every accomplished skier. To my knowledge, Harb is the first really to understand how skiing works, and he understands it so clearly that he is able to express it simply.

I spent 35 years working in ski resorts. I've directed ski schools in Arapahoe Basin, Vail, and Winter Park, Colorado, and in Coronet Peak, New Zealand. I managed ski school directors at Copper Mountain, Colorado, and Sugarloaf, Maine. I was president of the Professional Ski Instructors of America and the chief examiner of PSIA-Rocky Mountain. In that time I was a pretty good skier, but always only pretty good. I wanted to be better. I had access to the best ski teaching minds in the business and sought their help. And they were helpful, in varying degrees. But I was never able to achieve the breakthrough I intuitively knew was out there somewhere.

I met Harald in 1992 and we worked together for three years. In those three years I learned how to ski. Now, at age 60, I ski the best I ever did - perhaps not quite as athletically, but technically the way I always wanted to, the way I felt I could if I could just "get it". It's very satisfying.

Harald first aligned me. I am an "outside" skier, that is, bowlegged. I demonstrated all the classic adaptive moves of the bowlegged skier. Once aligned I could immediately feel all the things that I had been told to feel but which I never could. Next he showed me simple, fundamental skiing movements, and made me aware of the kinesthetic feedback from each movement. He put me in a different boot, a better boot for me. He made me foot beds. My skiing became precise, economical of movement. Inappropriate movements that I had fought for years to eliminate disappeared.

I have taught a lot of ski lessons, always using the best technical information available at the time. Many of my students learned very rapidly. Others did not, and I was disappointed and wondered where I had failed them; or was it that they did not try hard enough, or were lacking in motivation? I never felt that either of those was correct. **Now I know that they did not learn because they could not - they were *mechanically* incapable of performing the maneuvers.** Their biomechanical misalignment, and/or their inappropriate equipment, would not allow them to perform as they were being asked. Harald has now tested this with thousands of students and racers and the results have been dramatic. Properly aligned and equipped, skiers learn quickly to ski very well.

Shaped skis and modern boots and bindings are marvelous things. They are designed to carve beautiful narrow tracks in the snow. But different skiers need different skis and different boots. Some need risers and some should not have them. This book tells you which skiers need which skis and boots and risers. It also tells you how to use that great equipment so that you, too, can ski like you never have before. I hope that all who read this book benefit from Harald's understanding of our wonderful sport as much as I have.

Jerry Muth
September, 1997

Chapter 1 - Introduction

Skiing Unplugged

In the music world, Eric Clapton and MTV made the unplugged concept famous. Clapton, one of the best electric guitarists for decades, in this version performed live with acoustic instruments only. The performance received worldwide acclaim and awards. Many unplugged albums have followed, including ones from Nirvana and Pearl Jam. True quality and meaning of music is sometimes lost with all the over amplification and production. The roots and soul can be lost in the complex arrangements and instrumentation. In these unplugged performances, fundamental music is featured rather than being masked and "enhanced" by amps and production. In its simplicity lies the beauty of the performance.

In an effort to clear noise and get down to basic instruments, here is my unplugged version of skiing. In many fields, simple versions of a discipline are often more difficult to present than the complex. We have lived in the complex for so long that it has been accepted. Although skiers keep telling us that skiing is too technical and jargon-filled, until now it hasn't been unplugged. This book is designed to pull the plug on skiing. It presents the fundamentals that create expert skiing without extra distractions. It is written for the thousands of skiers who are or have been confused and stuck.

Initially, read it without trying to compare it to what you do now. Wait until you have tried to use the program as it is described. The information is different and requires thinking differently. By this I mean don't try to fit the new information into the framework of what you are using now or what you have been taught. Think about a new framework. Don't throw out all of what you have learned until now, but don't pass judgment. Try the program first and then make up your mind!

Tips on How to Use the Book

The book is divided into four parts:

Introduction:

     Reading the introduction is very important for all levels of skiers. It provides an explanation of this new approach to skiing and why it is so effective.

Skiing Progression:

     The skiing progression starts for the beginning skier and goes to the expert level. Enter the progression and practice it at any point. If the photos demonstrate your current skiing level, but you are stuck, use the bullet points as helpers. The bullets are at the end of each exercise. If you can perform every bullet you are ready to move to the next level of refinement. If you are having problems with the movements directed by the bullets, go back to the exercise where you can perform every bullet move. When you are able to perform all bullets moves in any particular exercise you are ready to move on. Reinforce the bullet moves to solidify your Primary Movements. Some fundamental movements presented in this method are not common ski movements, even for experts. Familiarize yourself with the new movements completely and the rest of the method will be easy to follow.

Alignment:

     The last section of the book is about alignment. If you find that some of the exercises are very difficult even after you have moved back two or even three exercises, you may be dealing with an alignment problem. If you recognize yourself in the descriptions of alignment problems read the alignment chapter.

Color Inserts:

     Cut the color inserts out of the book. They are helpful "pocket instructors" when skiing. The bullets correspond to the bullets in each chapter of the same exercise. They can be reminders for your daily ski refinement goals. Each card has two exercises. Choose the card with the exercises to suit your current performance level. Practice movements by referring to the pocket tips.

     There is also a glossary, on page 211. Look there if you find terms that are unfamiliar.

Primary Movements Teaching System

     The teaching system presented in this book is called the Primary Movements Teaching System™. It is based in scientific principles and employs the disciplines of physics, biomechanics, kinesiology, and anatomy to analyze movement in depth. Because the system relies so heavily on simplicity, accuracy of both the primary movements and resulting actions, whether complementary or detrimental, have been studied in depth. A great deal of emphasis has been placed on ensuring that all terms are used accurately, as language has created confusion in the past.

There are fundamental and significant differences between the Primary Movement Teaching System and other ski teaching systems:

The Primary Movements Teaching System is accurate and movement-based.
All movements in the Primary Movements Teaching System focus on creating and maintaining balance.

In order to achieve these proper movement patterns, the Primary Movements Teaching System begins with four goals:

Get the most out of your ski
All body movements must maximize ski design.

Focus on the feet
All movement must be analyzed starting at the feet, the base of the kinetic chain.

Accuracy and Efficiency
All movements must produce a defined result; extraneous movements are not primary, therefore they are inefficient or compensatory.

Balance
Simple, subtle, small, refined movements help the body to balance efficiently while skiing.

Many skiers use methods employing movements that disrupt balance, requiring constant compensation and offsetting actions. Typically, excessive movements start high in the kinetic chain at the hips and legs, disrupting balance.

> *"Primary Movements is a logical, common sense way to teach skiing. It makes skiing as easy to learn for my students as it was for me to make breakthroughs for my skiing that I didn't think possible at my age."*
> Bill Victory, Certified ski instructor

Explaining the Principles in the Primary Movements Teaching System

What is an expert skier? There are many skiers who consider themselves experts and they may well be, defined by the terrain they ski. I think that expert skiing is much more than skiing black diamond terrain. Real experts bring more to the table. Experts have the control and timing that enable them to meld one turn with the next. Watching an expert, you can see the connection between feeling and movement. Some experts sense the power and control produced by carving a ski in linked arcs;

others feel that their bodies float down the slope while their feet stay under them. These sensations bring joy and elegance to the skier. You must have developed your own idea of what an expert skier displays. My image is a skier moving in balance, flowing with the skis. The expert skier has a sense of flying down the mountain in complete control. The expert can let go to achieve the sense of exhilaration that only uncertainty can bring, yet plans well enough to know the skis will be in the right place for the next turn. Most skiers strive for this kind of skiing but few achieve it. They are hampered by inefficient movements, locked into a defensive style, and relegated to groomed green and blue slopes. When they do venture onto black runs, timidly, rigid terror dominates every move.

Have teaching systems contributed to stagnation in skiers? So many of the systems used by traditional ski teaching seem ineffective and wrought with low expectations, never changing or challenging the skier. Skiers aren't given credit for their ability to learn! The systems seem to teach below the ability of the students or teach down to a mediocre level, so skiers stay at the same level despite lessons. This may be because teaching has evolved to make the student feel satisfied with minimal or nonexistent improvement, or because the systems don't contain the tools to make improvement possible.

Not here, though. My philosophy differs greatly from this approach. If accurate movements producing desired outcomes are taught, if movements are presented in logical progressions, in small increments, and if they are based on the individual movement needs of the skier, then the skier will be successful immediately. Building and refining a progression that leads directly to an expressed goal saves time and frustration. If the teaching system is based on a progression of unconnected stages, movements, and rigid milestones or targets, it fulfills the needs of the system, not the student. These systems can only lead to frustration. Weighting both skis, positioning the feet in a wide stance, and turning both feet are some examples of what doesn't work. These actions don't develop balance. Granted, these systems give the skier a start, but directed down the road to terminal bad habits.

> *"Now I tip and carve the ski edge. I started skiing at 40 and it always puzzled me why my ski instructors would tell me to turn my foot and slide the tails of my skis. I always lost my balance. It just didn't make sense."*
> Jim Pitcock, MD

What if you already have bad habits, and they've been ingrained through past instruction? Not to worry, my approach teaches movements that produce technique to match your skiing ambition or goals. If you ski with the movements from this book you will be skiing with ease and balance. You will also develop great technique. Strength and athletic ability are not necessary to become expert. I have taught these methods to both instructors and recreational skiers, many of whom ski no more than eight days a season. They are now experts, and you can be too.

If you are a skier stuck in a dead-end movement pool, the culprit holding you back can usually be traced to the all important turn transition, at the point of edge change. Success or failure for most skiers can be linked to movements that create the edge change. This point in the turn produces most of the unsettling or unbalancing actions. There should be no point where balance is lost. Many skiers are taught to disrupt hard-earned balance at this stage by the overuse of rotary and twisting actions. The Primary Movements Teaching System is based on establishing a balanced position on the new support leg. You therefore start into the transition phase of the next turn already in balance, skiing with smooth turn connections and transitions. The ideal situation is to be in balance when it is time to let go of the old edge. Feeling stable and in balance is a great way to start a turn. What if you knew you could maintain balance and "relax to release" directly into the next turn without hesitation? Would you have the confidence to connect turn after turn floating down the mountain?

The start of the movement progression has elementary exercises. I use these basic movements daily to warm up and to refine balancing in my ski boots. Because the system has no dead-end, discarded movements, upper level skiers can use exercises at the first levels to hone their skills. The system teaches expert movements to beginners and intermediates with little emphasis on the stages or levels, called milestones, that restrict linear movement refinement. I don't teach wedge turns or wedge Christies, although a developing skier may achieve these maneuvers during the practice sessions. The goal is to teach and utilize accurate movements that take advantage of ski technology and direct you to parallel skiing.

Skis that sweep or windshield wiper the snow with their bases aren't being used as designed.

Skiers trained in Primary Movements move out and away from a wedge turn, never perfecting the arduous complexity of a wedge Christie only to discard it for a different requirement at the next level. I steer away from the pitfalls of limiting movements that direct a skier to slow progress. Systems that teach milestones and focus on stages in a progression plant you firmly in their quagmire. All of the chapters in this book teach movements that can be refined further. I believe in teaching movements to let the skis turn with minimal muscular effort. It can be done in an uncomplicated manner.

The three actions in skiing that, when performed properly, ground your skiing and establish the foundation for success are:

RELEASE, TRANSFER, ENGAGE

These three actions have specific roles in creating the transition from one turn to the next. When you start to focus on them in your skiing they will open the doors to a new way of skiing. I will introduce the movements to direct you to a clean, efficient edge change - an edge change without hesitation or snag that will free up your skiing. All of these actions start with the feet. I will break the movements into simple exercises so you can practice them at your level.

Traditionally, beginners and intermediates are taught movements that are completely different from those used by experts. For this reason, intermediates seldom become experts. An analysis of typical ski school sales records tell us that experts rarely take lessons, because lessons rarely improve their skiing. Many recreational skiers consider themselves to be experts and believe they ski better than most ski instructors do. Do you want to learn to ski using the systems that experts gave up on? I don't think so. We teach the movements that are used by only the best skiers. We introduce them in an easy, biomechanically sound progression.

After I stopped coaching racers, I started to train ski instructors. Many of the instructors were trying to ski like experts, emulating prescribed skiing models. However, these models espouse the same movements that are taught to intermediates. Daily on the slopes I see countless intermediate skiers with dead-end skills. You may have learned ineffective movements like rising toward the fall line, twisting your legs, and turning both feet while moving your body down the hill. Expert skiers do not use such movements. The instructors were having great difficulty making the connection between what they were teaching and how to use the same movements to improve their own skiing. It just wasn't happening. When I introduced accurate foot movements that taught ski engagement, they had huge breakthroughs.

In 1995, my boots and feet were on the cover of *Snow Country* magazine to introduce my article, "Focus on Your Feet". The article introduced the concepts I'd been coaching for twenty years. Use your feet as the first point for action.

All of the best coaches and instructors I know teach foot movements before refining technique with other parts of the body.

If your feet aren't working first, nothing you do with the upper body will make you an expert skier. Experts don't ski that way. Now you can learn how to focus on your feet to activate your skiing.

Kinetic Chain

Why is it that foot use leads to good balance? Foot movements in ski boots cause the ankle to react. The ankle then puts pressure on the sides of the boot. The side pressure stabilizes the ski and keeps it on a consistent edge. The ankle controls ski stability through the ski boot. If actions are started at the point closest to the ski-snow interface, movements can be small and refined. Foot movements start a reaction all the way up the body. The kinetic chain is a movement chain, starting at one end and transferring to the other. It is a series of actions or changes that reverberate through the body, initiated by a single primary or starter movement. It is particularly relevant when the primary movement is at the base of support or balance - the foot. The kinetic chain is explained in considerable detail in the alignment section (Chapter 12).

Stance Foot and Free Foot

The terms "stance foot" and "free foot" are used throughout the book. In an effort to avoid repetition, their use and meaning are described here. Skiing requires that the body be used in certain ways to create efficiency. Ski performance is better when one foot is dominant, hence the stance foot. A switch of foot responsibility occurs every time one turn is completed and a new one begins.

Stance Foot: *The foot that supports body balance*

The stance foot's responsibility is to support the body and establish a platform to stand against. Balance is focused on the stance foot and leg.

Free Foot: *The foot that initiates tipping and balancing actions*

The free foot's responsibility is to create desired turning actions. It supports little or sometimes no weight. The free foot is used to help control balance, and is moved "freely". Movements to begin turning are initiated by the free foot.

Shifting balance to the new stance foot is a deliberate movement. It consists of releasing and lifting the current stance foot. Once the current stance foot is lightened or lifted it is no longer the stance foot, hence the switch has been made.

The book devotes chapters, descriptions, and references to turn transitions. Note that when transition occurs it is always the stance foot that is lightened and released. In almost every case, the first movement to start a new turn is to lighten the stance foot. When you start to use these movements, balance and support shift automatically from one foot to the other.

Release: *Getting out of the old turn*

Parallel releasing actions are learned early, almost immediately, in the Primary Movements Teaching System experience. Learning to release using foot movement will develop functional balance in your skiing. Skiing with these movements focuses the mind so you can be aware of the sensations created. Awareness of ski edges and angles of skis to the snow will be part of your feedback. Releasing movements involving muscle relaxation to let gravity take you to the next turn will become part of your game plan. How would you feel if you had complete control of your body's downhill motion? If you are a beginner, you will build positive movement awareness. You avoid the bad habits that direct thousands of skiers towards terminal intermediate purgatory.

Balance Transfer: *Establishing a stance foot*

Commonly known as "weight transfer", we demonstrate an important distinction here that differentiates our program.

When you transfer "balance" you direct your action toward an outcome that creates a higher level of performance and the sensation of control.

Learning to balance on one ski is, to me, the most important principle in developing technique that permits rapid learning and limitless progress. Skiing dictates that we change our dominant stance leg as we initiate a new turn. Initiating a new turn begins while you are in the previous turn. This will assure an early, new, stance foot and more time to establish strong balance. Changing stance foot is critical for early balance in the new turn. This is a deliberate movement. It is to be performed assertively, not timidly. The exercises will show you how to perform the action of transfer. It can be done gradually and progressively, or instantaneously, depending on the skiing situation. Commitment to the movements that start the transfer of balance are key to the success of the next turn.

Early in our teaching system you will learn when and how to transfer stance and which foot to be on. If you can stand on your living room floor on one foot, you can learn to ski like an expert. When it is time to change to a new stance foot you simply pick up or lift the present stance foot off the snow. The former stance foot now becomes the free foot.

Engage: *Tipping the skis to create a new turn*

The easiest action of the three is engaging, because you have already started this action by performing the correct releasing and transferring movements. Engaging is more of a controlling activity. It determines how quickly or aggressively you start into the next turn. Through simple use of the free foot you will be able to control not only the length of the turn, but also the speed at which it develops. Engaging becomes automatic once free foot activity controls the entry to the turn.

There are no mysteries to good skiing, just accurate, efficient, effective movements.

Balancing

All of the movements discussed above require a crucial underlying ability, balance. Balancing is the most misunderstood and neglected action in skiing. Most skiers never realize what balance is or where it comes from because they have never been properly introduced to it. I am talking about a different level of balance, a higher standard.

Balance means many things to different people. For the victim of a severe head injury, standing upright and walking can demonstrate phenomenal balance. We wouldn't expect that person to be skiing. His balance has not developed to a point where he is ready for further, more complex movement. In the same way, I don't adhere to the standard that defines balanced skiing as the ability to stand on two skis while moving down the mountain. For an expert skier, this is not enough balancing ability. My standard of balance is the ability to stand and ski on one foot. The program you are about to learn develops one-footed balancing ability. It challenges the skier to improve and increase balancing ability in small logical easy steps. Don't be discouraged - balance has been studied in detail. The results show that humans can increase their balancing ability dramatically if training is applied.

In the past four years this program has created dramatic skiing improvement by introducing one-footed skiing. You will experience balance training as you try the movements in this system. You will also be trained to balance on one foot when you need it to do advanced maneuvers.

Use the Ski's Shape

I want to discuss ski use early in the book because it will help clear up much of the confusion that clouds skiing. We have all heard that turn roundness or shape plays a large part in speed control. All expert skiers have the ability to control speed at will, because they have a round turn built into their technique. Conversely, faulty technique makes efforts to control speed miserable and frustrating. It's the old cart before the horse thing: you won't manage a round turn with improper technique. It has always frustrated me to watch skiers being introduced to rounding turns before they have the ability to do so. Traditional skiing dictates that we teach students "shaping" to bring about round turns. I have tried unsuccessfully to find the "shaping" muscle in my anatomy books. How, then, is the skier supposed to perform this shaping action? With the Primary Movements Teaching System, I present specific methods to build a round turn. So, let's take the mystery out of shaping. Shaping or turn shape is completely dependent on how you use the ski. Skidding the turn will never give you shape. Once skidding starts, the control you desire disappears. Skidding results from foot steering and from hip and leg twisting actions. Once in motion, these actions are especially hard to slow, counteract, or control on the new shaped skis.

If skidding were an effective way to control speed, all experts would skid their way down the mountain.

If skiers really wanted to learn how to skid, I would have devoted my career to developing nifty ways to teach it. I have never had a student come to me, having mastered carving, asking to learn how to improve his or her skidding. Carving a round turn is dependent on how and when the ski is angled to the snow, the amount of pressure applied, and the flexing characteristics and sidecut (side profile) of the ski. Complicated, of course - that's why round, carved turns are so elusive. I will describe how, with simple movements, to develop round turns and to create turn shape in the chapters devoted to teaching the Primary Movements.

Shaped Skis

Recent developments in ski design have had a profound effect on our ability to make round turns. Sharper, rounder, and deeper turns are possible on the modern shaped skis. Probably the most significant advantage of shaped skis is carving with a gently tipped, low edge angle. The technology makes it easier to turn, control, and direct the skis with small tipping movements. As a result, ski teaching can take advantage of a huge technological breakthrough that benefits beginning skiers.

Leg turning or twisting is the most common gross skiing movement, used for years to generate direction changes. This is still the case in the most current teaching manuals. The origin of ski methods using twisting can be traced to Austrian systems and the George Joubert books of the Sixties, when skis were heavy and stiff, men were men, and you had to be a real man to turn the skis. If the equipment has changed significantly since that era, why hasn't technique kept up the pace?

That's why I came up with Primary Movements, a sophisticated approach designed for this generation of new skis. Now you can ski with less energy and have more fun, control, and balance. As with most good things, though, there are the qualifiers. You can't use the old skiing system with the new skis. I have personally watched hundreds of skiers test the new shaped skis. About fifty percent of the skiers come back from the experience proclaiming the virtues of the new designs, saying things like, "These skis are so easy to turn", and "They really carve, I can feel the carving." The other fifty percent have mixed reactions. Their comments are less enthusiastic: "No big difference" or "My current skis feel more stable." The reason for these seemingly contradictory reactions is the variety of ways the skiers propel the skis into a turn. The need for adaptive movements by the skiers because of alignment irregularities often adds another ingredient to the less than positive reaction to the new skis. Simply put, people who don't like the new, shaped skis don't know how to use them. Consider applying the steering energy needed to turn a huge dump truck to a precise, light, sports car like a Mazda Miata. The car would either overturn, roll, or go off the road. Similarly, applying the turning energy needed to fling conventional skis into a turn to a shorter, lighter, shaped ski will yield unexpected and unpleasant results.

Many traditional skiers are reluctant to embrace the new technology skis. They have perfected a way of skiing over thirty years, and now they find the new skis don't live up to their billing. I can make an analogy to the big sized tennis rackets, remembering my summers as a young tennis pro, how the good players were too cool to use those "cheater" rackets. It didn't take them long to realize that the rackets provided much more power and higher performance with less effort.

The skiing traditionalist will come to the same conclusion: learn faster, more easily, with less fatigue, and have more fun. Their skiing will also adapt to become more efficient, accurate, and less forceful. If you want to take a shaped ski lesson, be careful. Ask specifically for an instructor who skis on shaped skis and has taught on them for more than a full season. Many instructors will be trying to apply the old teaching techniques to the new skis. In my opinion, this will produce limited success. It's like using your word processor with only the knowledge that came from using the typewriter. It can work, but the potential is never realized. This is presently the only teaching system specifically for the shaped skis. More details about shaped skis and selection are in the alignment chapter.

Chapter 2 - First Moves

"The lost arts of skiing"

Primary movements, including stance and free foot use and accompanying lateral movements, are presented here. The movements are introduced in ski boots without skis. Foot use is easiest to sense for the first time in this simple, nonthreatening environment. All primary movements start as close to the ground as possible using small foot and ankle movements, developing balance. The movements in these exercises form the basis of top level skiing. Consequently, even skiers who are beyond novice level should not overlook them. I urge experts to review these early primary movements and use them as a refresher.

I have introduced primary movements to experts on many occasions. Although these movements are not difficult, many experts have difficulty performing them. It is not unusual for experts to struggle with their skiing because foot tipping was neglected at a crucial time in their skiing development. I continue to surprise experts by making their skiing smoother and more graceful, enhancing their finesse by focusing on foot and ankle movements.

You can quickly develop these abilities in a safe, on-snow practice session with this logical, concise movement system. The movement series must be performed with great attention to precision. If you are accurate with the movements you will maximize your connection between how you learn movements and the sensations that enable you to reproduce them. Although everyone may experience sensations differently, sensations are best developed through accurate movement patterns. In this manner, you guarantee meaningful sensations early in the progression.

Lateral foot and boot movements develop edge awareness. When you identify the sides of the boot soles by sensing them with your feet you can begin to control the edging angles. Everyday I ski, I find opportunities to practice these movements before I go on skis. In the lodge or in the parking area, if I have my boots on, I constantly tip my feet to identify the movements and sense the boot edges. I find it interesting to observe the reaction of the upper legs and hips initiated by foot-tipping movements. This reaction to foot movement by the mid- and upper body demonstrates the kinetic chain discussed in Chapter 1. I then transfer the movement awareness developed in boots to my on-snow skiing needs. The subtle increasing and decreasing of the ski's angle to the snow, so essential to skiing refinement, is developed by increased foot awareness.

These exercises help the first time skier achieve the goal of developing balance for when skis will be used. Rather than being a slippery device that unexpectedly shoots out from under you, the ski will become a more predicable, trustworthy friend.

Movement progression starts on following page

Previous: *Introduction*

2-1.   Tipping the feet on level terrain

Next: *Tipping on a sidehill*

a   *b*   *c*

Fig. 2-1. Tipping the feet in boots only, on level terrain

It is natural for most beginning skiers to feel uncomfortable. Opportunities to boost self-esteem are rare in first time skiing experiences. Here is a chance to experience standing like an expert on your first day. Here are the positions and sensations that experts feel. Every step of the movement progression provides achievable movement increments, therefore you can feel progress. A positive self image from your first time experience is key to success.

In Brief

Stand on a flat and level surface with the feet close, but not quite touching. Point the feet straight ahead, not pigeon or duck toed. Roll the feet from side to side in order to tip the boots from one edge to the other. Move slowly to make sure that the angles the boots form with the snow are the same for both feet.

Details

Fig. a. Stand evenly weighted with boots flat on the snow.

Fig. b. Roll or tip your feet slightly to the right. Stand on the big toe edge of the left boot, and the little toe edge of the right boot. Balance evenly on both feet, but spread your poles wide to provide some security.

Fig. c. Increase your foot tipping to greater lower leg angles to the right. Move as far as possible without losing balance or falling over.

Fig. d. Return to this neutral stance.

Fig. e. Now go in the opposite direction. Tip your feet slightly to the left. Feel weight on the little toe edge of the left foot, and the big toe edge of the right foot. By tipping your feet even further to the left, you achieve greater angles.

Summary

In these photos, the lower legs show angles to the snow and the knees are moved out toward the side. Let the knees follow foot movement. By starting the movements at the feet, the rest of the body will adjust to maintain balance. Again, this is the kinetic chain, so let it work.

d   *e*   *f*

Try this exercise indoors facing a mirror or outdoors with a friend watching to make sure that both feet tip to the same angle. The lower legs should remain parallel throughout the tipping. Relax at the hips; let the knees bend freely so foot actions can produce changes up the body. If the knees end up closer together than the feet, focus on the foot being tipped toward the little toe side. If the knees end up with a larger gap between them than the feet, focus on the foot being tipped toward the big toe. Difficulty with tipping one way or the other could indicate an alignment problem.

A common misconception upon seeing this exercise is that the knees must be pushed from side to side. Do not use the upper leg muscles as the driving force behind the movement practiced here, as they initiate femur rotation. The feet should be your focus because they are the most direct connection to the boots and skis, and give the most feedback in sensing balance.

Be careful that the boots do not pivot on the snow. The toes should continue to point straight ahead while the feet roll from edge to edge. Knocking excess snow off the boot soles before beginning the exercise will help.

Notice the similarities between an actual, dynamic carved ski turn leg position and the position created in this skiing movement.

Bullets

- Point both boots straight ahead (not toes directed in or out)
- Primary movement: tip feet from one side to the other
- Keep both boots at the same angle to the snow

Previous: *Tipping the feet on level terrain*

2-2.   **Tipping on a sidehill**

Next: *Tipping with the free foot*

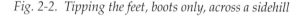

a   *b*   *c*

Fig. 2-2. Tipping the feet, boots only, across a sidehill

The movements of tipping demonstrated are done standing across the hill, to produce the feeling of edging you sense with skis. These exercises introduce you to sensations of the sides of the feet in boots. Almost all foot actions that create ski turn transitions can be traced back to this movement series. This is similar to the previous exercise, except that it is performed on a gentle slope.

In Brief

Stand with your feet pointed across the hill. Keep your boots parallel. Tip and roll your feet from side to side in order to get the boots from one edge to the other. Move slowly, and make sure that your shins remain parallel. Try this exercise facing both directions on the hill.

Details

Fig. a. Stand balanced more on the stance foot (skier's left). Because of the slope, the boot soles are at a slight angle to the snow. You'll be standing on the little toe edge of the uphill, free foot (skier's right) and the big toe edge of the stance foot.

Fig. b. Roll or tip feet up the slope to edge the boots to the snow. Tip both feet evenly to achieve similar angles. Balance using your feet, but spread the poles, hands, and arms for added security.

Fig. c. Tip your feet further to greater angles. Stay evenly balanced on both feet. Tip as far as possible without losing your balance.

Fig. d. Tip your feet towards downhill, passing through the starting stance.

Fig. e. Tip your boots farther downhill, shifting balance toward the downhill foot.

d   *e*   *f*

Fig. f. Stand on the little toe edge of the downhill foot (skier's left) and the big toe edge of the uphill foot (skier's right).

Summary

Relax the hips so that the legs may follow the movement started by the feet. Have a friend watch to see that you tip both feet to the same angle. Notice how *fig. c* looks similar to the finish of a parallel turn.

Difficulty in tipping the feet evenly may demonstrate an alignment problem. The knock-kneed skier will find the knees touching, while the bowlegged skier will find the knees spread wider than the feet.

Keep the boots from twisting or pivoting on the snow. Keep them facing straight ahead throughout the tipping. Keep the pelvis stable and facing forward.

Bullets
- Use wide arm position and stick pole tips in the snow for balance
- Tip feet in both directions up and down the slope

Previous: *Tipping on a sidehill*

2-3.   Tipping with the free foot

Next: *Walking the "S" line*

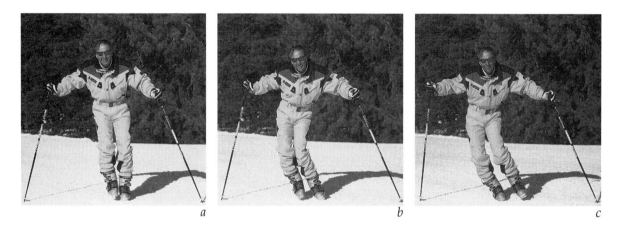

a   *b*   *c*

Fig. 2-3. Tipping the feet, boots only, alternating stance and free foot

This exercise builds on the previous exercises by clearly distinguishing between the stance foot and free foot. It is helpful to create some tension between the legs by pressing them together. Practice this movement in both directions. If you can perform these movements in ski boots the way they are described below, you can be an expert quickly. Don't wait until winter; practice these movements at home on a carpet. Be careful that the poles don't slip, because you will need them for balance. You might try this in a hallway or doorway where you can reach both sides with your hands, using the walls instead of poles for balance.

In Brief

Stand sideways on the hill, feet aimed straight ahead and close together. Lift the uphill, free foot and tip it as far as you can toward the little toe side. Let the downhill, stance foot follow the tipping of the free foot. Once both feet are tipped as far as possible, place the free foot back on the snow, and lift the stance foot. This will require the assistance of the poles for balance. Now tip the new free foot (skier's left) toward its little toe side.

Details

Fig. a. The downhill foot (skier's left) is the stance foot. Balance entirely on this foot. Pick up the uphill foot (skier's right). It is the free foot. It will lead the tipping movement.

Fig. b. Start tipping the free foot and balance on the stance foot. Let the stance leg tip to the same angle as the free foot.

Fig. b & c. The free foot is tipped as far as possible, and the stance foot is tipped to the same angle. The stance foot is tipped onto its big toe edge, and the rest of the body complements this tipping in order to maintain balance.

d   *e*   *f*

Fig. d. Transfer balance from stance to free foot. Place the free foot (the skier's right) on the snow on its little toe edge. Lift the stance foot (the skier's left). Make sure you are balancing on the little toe edge of the uphill foot.

Fig. e. After establishing balance on the new stance foot, tip the free foot (skier's left) to its little toe edge.

Fig. f. The stance foot will roll from its little toe edge to flat. Tip the free foot even further, keep the shins parallel, and the stance foot will roll onto its big toe edge.

Summary

This exercise practices the movements of releasing the old turn and engaging a new turn.

Lead the tipping movement with the free foot. Make sure that both feet are tipped to the same angle.

The stance foot should maintain balance as its primary role. When switching the stance and free foot, make sure that the new stance foot is placed on the snow on its little toe edge.

Difficulties in maintaining the same angle from the free foot to the stance foot can indicate an alignment problem.

Even at this introductory level, the movements practiced are integral to expert skiing.

Bullets

- Use poles for balance
- Pick up free foot
- Balance on stance foot
- Tip free foot toward the little toe side

2-4.   Walking the "S" line

a

b

Fig. 2-4. *Stepping around the 'S' curve in the snow*   *c*

In Brief

Walking and tipping the feet while moving through the shape of a turn provides sensations of proper body use. On a gentle hill, use your pole to draw an "S" shape on the snow. Stand at the top of the "S", straddling the line with both feet tipped toward the slope. Lift the downhill foot to make it the free foot. Tip it onto its little toe edge, and then set it down on the snow along the "S" line. Lift the uphill foot off of its little toe edge. Set it down along the line on its big toe edge. Continue to step along the "S" line while keeping one foot on its big toe edge, and the other on its little toe edge. The movements developed here give you feedback about how foot movements control and position the upper body and legs.

Details

Fig. a. Both feet are tipped or rolled uphill. The skier's right foot is on its big toe edge, the left on its little toe edge.

Fig. a & b. Lift the right foot so it becomes the free foot. Tip it toward its little toe edge. Tip the stance foot (skier's left) toward its big toe edge to follow the lead of the free foot.

Fig. b. Tip the stance foot (skier's left) to a flat position on the snow.

Fig. c. Tip the free foot further toward the little toe, and roll the stance foot over so that the body is balanced on its big toe side.

Fig. d. Place the right foot on the snow on its little toe edge to maintain the angle of tip. Pick up the left foot (keeping it tipped) then set it farther along the "S" line on its big toe edge.

Fig. e & f. Step one foot after the other, always setting the feet on the correct edge, while following the "S" curve.

d

e

f

Summary

When you have your skis on and you perform these movements your skis will slide and turn through this arc. In boots, you must step to move around the "S" curve.

The crucial moment in this exercise is the transition from one direction and set of edges to the other, *fig. a* to *fig. b*. Making the first movements starts you into the new turn. If, instead, you pick up the left foot and aim it in the direction of the "S" curve, you will get a wedge (snowplow). Small or large, the wedge is an undesirable feature that's best avoided.

During each step around the curve, keep the feet tipped on edge. Avoid aiming the toes at the curve. Again, this action will lead to a wedge.

Bullets
- Use poles for balance
- Tip free foot
- Alternate balance from little toe to big toe edge

2-5.   Lift & tip free foot with skis

a   *b*   *c*

Fig. 2-5. Tipping the feet and skis across a sidehill; alternating stance and free foot

Shaped skis give skiers the opportunity to balance and learn quickly. I use shaped skis in all of these demonstrations. If you can perform the balancing movements introduced here you will develop parallel skiing movements. Some skiers will take longer than others to develop these movements, but it is important to introduce them for they are primary to efficient skiing. As in exercises 2-2 and 2-3 done without skis, the idea is to sense the edges with the soles and sides of your feet. Being on skis doesn't change that goal. Doing these exercises with skis does present some interesting new challenges. The difference will be the skis' tendency to slide forward and back. It is important that both skis be exactly ninety degrees to the vertical slope line (called the fall line). This position will keep you from sliding forward or backward. This exercise introduces lateral movements and one footed balance with skis. You will be using all four edges of your skis. Advanced skiers rarely learned to use all four edges. You are learning expert movements and balancing techniques.

In Brief

Pick a gentle spot near the bottom of the slope. Use your arms with the poles in the snow to help maintain balance. Feel that each arm supports you equally. With slightly more weight on the downhill or stance foot, tip your feet up the slope to make the edge of the ski bite into the snow. The right foot should be lifted, free from the snow, while the downhill foot's big toe side should feel most of your balance. Tip back and forth slightly from a comfortable initial stance on that foot before you go to the fully tipped position. Remember, start all lateral movements with your free foot. Relax to allow your legs to move in the hip joints.

Note: the shading in the photos indicates the stance side.

Details

Fig. a. Both feet are already tipped to full range. Try to feel most of the balance on the stance foot. Continue to tip the free foot toward its little toe side to assure that your lower legs stay parallel.

d   *e*   *f*

Fig. b & c. From a normal, comfortable stance, pick up your uphill foot; it is now the free foot (skier's right). Slowly tip the stance foot to its big toe side. Once you have tipped the ski as far as possible, slowly rock the foot back and forth on and off its edge.

Fig. d. Switch back to a two footed stance.

Fig. e. Pick up the downhill ski (skier's left) so it becomes the free foot; the stance foot is now the uphill ski. Tip the new stance foot (uphill) toward its little toe side. Balance as long on it as long as you can. Practice this action numerous times or until you can balance comfortably.

Summary

These exercises, although initiated by foot movements, will involve the turning of the upper legs in the pelvis. While you are on the edges keep the pelvis as stable and motionless as possible. Try to keep all the movement below a stable pelvis. If you can control this part of the body you will already be far beyond the development of most intermediate skiers.

Bullets

- Stand ninety degrees to the vertical fall line
- Pick up one ski
- Tip the stance ski on and off an edge
- Switch to the other stance foot and repeat

Previous: *Lift & tip free foot with skis*
2-6.   Stepping tips in a circle
Next: *Side stepping*

a   *b*   *c*

Fig. 2-6. Stepping ski tips in fan pattern on level area

The purpose of these stepping actions is to learn to change direction. The stepping action puts the skis on a slight edge and develops balance and independent foot movement.

In Brief

Move the front or tips of the skis, one foot at a time, in either direction. Take small steps to allow for control, quickness, and balance. You will be moving from one foot to the other, changing balance, as the ski tips trace the outside or circumference of a circle. Pole use is important to help maintain balance. Start slowly on a flat area and move your poles as the body turns.

Details

Fig. a. Get started with a narrow stance and comfortable hand position supported by the poles.

Fig. b. Move the left ski tip to the left. Keep the tail of the ski stationary. The left ski is now closer to the left pole. Move the pole to maintain an equal distance from pole to hips as you step further to the left.

Fig. c. Step the right ski tip over to a parallel matching position with the left. Continue to move in this manner producing at least six steps.

Fig d. Move the right pole closer to maintain balance and symmetrical hand position.

Fig. e & f. The stepping continues in a slow fluid manner coordinating hand and foot movement. When you reach a position forty-five degrees from the start, begin the same movements, starting with the right ski tip, in the opposite direction to achieve a full ninety-degree direction change.

d   *e*   *f*

Summary

Although these movements seen repetitive after the first few steps, they must be done accurately to prevent the skis from crossing or stepping on the poles. The ski tips should move no more than about twelve inches at a time. The idea is to establish solid balance over the stance foot before moving. Notice how the body is always comfortably balanced while the free foot is off the snow.

Bullets

- Step one ski tip to the side
- Match or complement the step by bringing the other ski parallel
- Move the poles to complement the foot movements

Previous: *Stepping tips in a circle*
2-7A.   Side stepping
Next: *Stepping tips to turn*

Before trying the next exercise it may be useful to practice side stepping up a gentle slope. Side stepping is similar to walking sideways up a staircase, one step at the time. Make sure that both feet are on the same step before taking the next step. Start from the same position you did in exercise 2-5. Lift and tip as you step your free foot up the slope. Keep your ski edge of the stance foot in the snow as you step. Once you achieve a position on the slope about five feet from the bottom, hold your poles firmly in the snow and step your tips ever so gradually and slightly down into the slope. When you feel the tug of gravity wanting to pull your skis let yourself go. Standing balanced on the center or over the middle of the ski, pull the poles out of the snow. You will slide slowly back to the bottom of the slope. As you become comfortable with this exercise, move on to the next.

Bullets
- Side step up the slope
- Stand on an edged ski as you move the other
- Hold yourself in position with your poles
- Step your ski tips down the slope to begin moving

Previous: *Side stepping*
2-7B.   Stepping tips to turn
Next: *Stepping garland*

Although you will be standing on one ski for only a short time as you step, it is long enough for the ski to react to the pressure developed on it. Shaped skis will often turn while you are stepping from foot to foot. This may be your first experience riding on a turning ski. If the ski doesn't turn for you, don't worry - conditions may not be just right yet. Turning conditions depend on the kind of ski, speed, grade of slope, and type of snow. The exercise may not yield a turning ski on the first try but it is still important as a building block in your quest toward parallel skiing.

In Brief

On a slight incline, aim your skis at an angle down the slope (toward the fall line). The solid arrow on the page always indicates the fall line. It is the direction of the strongest pull of gravity. Allow your skis to slide down the slope. As you gradually start to slow, or as soon as you feel comfortable, use the stepping movements as practiced in exercise 2-6, "Stepping tips in a circle", to change direction gradually. Combining movements you developed in the last series of exercises, step to a slight edge as you move the ski tip up the hill. As in exercise 2-5, shading indicates the stance side.

Fig. 2-7B. Stepping up from shallow traverse

Details

Fig. a. From a stable, balanced stance with weight equally balanced on both feet, start a straight run down the fall line.

Fig. b. Depending on the terrain, you can start to step the right foot to the right almost immediately after you begin moving. To take the first step you must pick up the right foot and balance on the left. Pick up and move the front of the ski as you did in the stepping exercise.

Fig. c. As the free foot and ski are placed on the snow, balance on that foot. Then step the stance foot back to parallel. Use smaller and frequent steps to yield positive results.

Fig. d. Step the right foot, and balance on it. Pick up the left foot and bring it to parallel.

Summary

Try to get as much direction change in the distance available with the smallest steps. The result of these movements is an engagement of the shaped skis. If the left ski starts turning on its own in the direction you are stepping (in this case to the right), enjoy the ride. As the skis turn you will slow your speed. All these movements "focus on the feet". The upper body stays very still as in all the exercises. If you need the poles for balancing aids you can drag them or hold them lifted at your side as demonstrated in the photos.

Bullets
- Step the right ski tip up the slope
- Balance from one foot to the next as you step around the turn

---

Previous: *Stepping tips to turn*

2-8.   Stepping garland

Next: *Eliminating the wedge*

Consider this exercise as an extension of exercise 2-7. This exercise format in skiing is called a step garland. The word garland refers to following the shape of decorative half turns - linked semicircles that drape across the hill. The purpose of the exercise is to become familiar with moving down the slope with your ski tips (the direction indicated by the arrow in fig. 2-7) without actually going "all the way around the corner." As your ski tips head down the slope you will pick up speed; step the tips back up the slope if you want to slow down. The exercise helps you to practice movements that reinforce direction changes utilizing the design of shaped skis.

In Brief

Make stepping movements in directions both up the slope and down the slope. Pick terrain where you have room to practice. A wide slope with few skiers is preferable.

In Detail

Begin as for exercise 2-7. From a stable, balanced stance with weight equally distributed on both feet, start to slide down the slope at a shallow angle. Step the skis uphill (as in fig. 2-7) until you create a direction change back into the slope. As the skis move back across and up the slope and speed is reduced, start to step the skis back down the slope. As the skis aim down you will pick up speed. Once you feel that you are headed down far enough, step the tips back up the slope, to reduce speed.

Summary

As in the previous exercise, make numerous, small steps rather than large ones. Practice several times, stepping the skis slightly further down the slope each time before stepping back up. It's preferable to be comfortable with uphill stepping for speed control before you venture too steeply down the slope.

Bullets
- Step ski tips down the slope
- Step back up to reduce speed
- Repeat as you move across the slope

The charts on the following pages describe how alignment affects the results of some of the exercises in this chapter. Consult Chapter 12, Alignment, for additional details.

Maneuver	Knock-Kneed	Correctly Aligned	Bowlegged
2-1. In boots, no skis, standing on flat terrain. Tip boots from edge to edge. Try to achieve same angle with both feet.	It will be difficult for the foot tipping toward the little toe to tip as far as the foot tipping toward the big toe. This creates the "knees together" appearance.	Both boots will tip to the same angle. The shins will stay parallel.	It's difficult to tip the foot toward the big toe edge. At the transition from one side to the other, the knees will appear farther apart than the feet (bowlegged).
2-2. In boots, no skis, standing on a gentle incline with boots pointed across the hill. Using the feet and ankles, roll the boots until their soles are horizontal and bite into the snow.	Rolling the uphill boot onto the little toe edge will be difficult. The knees will end up closer together than the feet.	The boots can be rolled with equal ease to reach the same angle on the hill. The shins remain parallel through the rolling.	It's difficult to keep the knees together. The downhill foot will be flatter to the snow than the uphill foot. The uphill foot tips easily to the little toe edge.
2-3b. In boots, no skis, standing across the fall line on a gentle incline. Balance on the downhill foot. Roll that foot onto its big toe edge. Use the poles as balance aids.	The skier will likely stand with the knees pressed together and the hips flexed and lowered. The boot sole will gain very little edge angle to the snow.	The correctly aligned skier can stand normally and balance with a slightly flexed leg. The free leg can be held almost parallel to the stance leg, and the free boot sole will be tilted to the same angle as the stance boot.	It's difficult to maintain balance on the edged, downhill foot. Maintaining balance requires moving the free foot away from the body. The arms will be extended and the leg will be straight.
2-4. Walking around the "S" path in the snow.	A knock-kneed position will be evident in almost every step. It's very difficult for the skier to roll the foot to the little toe edge in the transition from turn to turn. The knee of the big-toe-edged foot will point toward and touch the leg of the little-toe-edged foot.	In the transition from one direction to the other, the angles of the boot soles will match. The lower legs will remain parallel throughout the tipping.	A bowlegged position with space between the knees will be evident throughout the exercise. The knee of the free leg will seem to bow out away from the body as it tips to the little toe edge. It will be difficult to tip the outside leg toward the big toe edge.

Maneuver	Knock-Kneed	Correctly Aligned	Bowlegged
With skis, standing on a flat surface. Tip the skis from one side to the other, keeping both skis at the same angle to the snow.	It will be difficult to tip the ski to the little toe edge. This creates the "knees together", "A-frame" appearance.	Both boots will tip to the same angle. The shins will stay parallel.	It's difficult to tip the ski toward the big toe edge. At the transition from one side to the other, the knees will appear farther apart than the feet (bowlegged).
2-6. Stepping ski tips in a circle.	The skis will tend to stay on their big toe edges. The knees will touch when the feet are apart.	The skis will stay fairly flat on the snow throughout the stepping.	The little toe edge of the skis will often catch or snag on the snow. The stance foot might slip when you step off of it. The knees are further apart than the feet.
On a gentle incline, sidestep up the slope about three steps.	Sidestepping is difficult. The downhill foot, on its big toe edge, often doesn't grip the snow. The uphill ski stays flat on the snow; it's not rolled onto its little toe edge.	Both skis grip the snow and provide a stepping platform, the uphill on its little toe edge, the downhill on its big toe edge.	It's difficult to balance on the downhill foot without leaning the body uphill or spreading the feet apart. The downhill foot sometimes slips when you push off of it.
2-7. Stepping tips to turn.	It's difficult to step to the little toe edge of the uphill ski and to balance on this foot, so stepping the stance foot over to match is often slow and late. The stance ski often runs straight down the hill rather than gently curving.	Both skis can be edged to the snow, and you can balance on either foot. The exercise is easy to complete in either direction.	The stance ski often slips just as you push off of it. You often lean into the slope to step the foot toward the little toe edge.

Chapter 3 - Eliminate the Wedge

The chapter that transforms the terminal intermediate to a parallel skier, with critical movements that benefit all levels of skiers

Skiing really starts to be fun when your skis are parallel. No matter what anyone says, real skiing is done with skis parallel. You haven't experienced the potential of your skiing until you can link parallel turns, at least three in a row. This chapter is here to help you eliminate the pitfalls that riddle skiing progress. It will lead you away from wedge turn and wedge Christie maneuvers. Many of you already know how difficult it is to break the wedge habit. It seems that once skis learn the wedge they never want to let it go. Your legs and skis seem to spring automatically into a wedge position in every situation. Move away from those dead-end, inefficient movements. The Primary Movements Teaching System doesn't acknowledge that the wedge exists as a station in skiing progressions, therefore the wedge is renamed. A more appropriate name is derived from the more common use of the maneuver. Call it the LMD, or liftline maneuvering device.

The Primary Movements Teaching System doesn't teach a wedge - it goes directly to parallel movements. However, there are many dedicated, aspiring skiers stuck in a wedge. This chapter gets rid of it. Primary movements will move you away from the wedge.

The wedge makes skiers dependent on using opposing edges - at all times, the two skis are fighting each other. Both feet are tipped toward the big toe edge. Primary movements introduce you to skiing using all four edges of the skis. A priority is to develop balance and a "stance foot." Establishing balance on the stance foot is the key to breaking wedge dependence.

Many traditionalists will respond by throwing up their hands and uttering "impossible, it can't be done." Trust yourself and the new skis. Leave the old, frustrating ways behind. Modern ski equipment and primary movements give you a big advantage.

Parallel movements are taught early to avoid ingraining what will be discarded. In the process of learning parallel movements, you may inadvertently make wedge turns or even wedge Christies, but that is not the goal. Make note of these results, as they are part of the process, but direct your efforts to performing the accurate, correct movements. Substituting other components from previous methods of skiing may confuse your new movement ability. Focus on the simplicity of the primary movements to avoid confusion.

Previous: *Stepping garland*

3-1.   Free foot move

Next: *Stationary wedge to free foot closure*

a   *b*   *c*

Fig. 3-1. Use a solid stance to practice free foot movements

In Brief

With the downhill ski removed and a ski on the uphill foot, stand across the slope. In this exercise, the downhill foot is the stance foot and the uphill foot is the free foot. Because the stance foot is without a ski, it will be a solid platform. Anchor yourself on the stance foot. Use your poles to assist in balancing. Move the back of the free ski up and down the slope until you can tip the foot to the little toe side as it approaches the stance foot.

Details

Fig. a. Place the stance foot firmly in the snow and balance on it. Move the back or tail of the free ski up the slope. Keep the tip of the free ski in place.

Fig. b-d. Draw the free foot with a light brushing action on the snow toward the stance foot. As the ski starts to move closer, focus on tipping the free foot toward the little toe edge. Sense the contact of the little toe edge against the snow.

Fig. e. Once the skis are parallel, i.e. the feet are almost touching, tip the free foot toward its little toe side.

Summary

Repeat the movements several times, changing skis and direction to familiarize yourself with the movement on both sides of the body. Balance on the stance foot, keeping the free foot lightly on the surface of the snow. Exaggerate the action of tipping toward the little toe edge as the ski approaches the stance leg. Develop the foot inverter muscles to flatten and tip the free ski to the little toe

d   e

side. Familiarize yourself completely with this feeling. When performing this movement while skiing, the free foot will create direction changes for the stance ski. You are now using expert movements to bring balance to your skiing.

Bullets
- Balance on the stance foot
- Tip the free foot from its big toe edge to its little toe edge
- Draw the free foot toward the stance foot

3-2. Stationary wedge to free foot closure

Using primary movements, you can experience the movements that balance the body.

Free foot use depends greatly on how well you stand and balance on your stance foot. In the previous exercise we were able to focus completely on the free foot because we had the stability and traction of a ski boot in the snow. Here, you must divide your attention slightly. The stance foot has a ski on it, which presents new challenges. It can slip down, forward, or backward when you stand on it.

This exercise is similar to exercise 2-5 but rather than tipping you are drawing the free ski in toward the stance foot. Use the same lateral tipping movements of the stance foot you learned in Chapter 2 to establish a comfortable stance. Try to feel pressure building along the whole inside or big toe edge of the stance foot, indicating that your ski has its edge in the snow. Sense the changes in your body as you lighten the free foot. Use small movements of the stance foot to adjust your balance. The kinetic chain working through your body will create balance and align with your stance foot.

d

e

Most teaching systems try to create positions, rather than providing movements for balance. Examples would be "move your shoulders down the hill", or "tip your upper body toward the lodge." These methods attempt to achieve a position, but they don't create balance for the skier. They overlook the imbalance that could be the reason for the skier's "incorrect" body position.

In Brief

Use a slope with a slight incline and stand near the bottom. Make sure you are standing exactly ninety degrees to the fall line. Use your poles for support while you make sure the stance foot is firmly tipped in the snow. Pick up the free foot and stand solely on the stance foot. Make sure you are balancing comfortably. Keep the tips of the skis together and move the tail of the free foot up the slope. From the wedged position, flatten and pull the free foot toward the stance foot.

Details

Fig. a. Lighten the free foot and move the tail up the slope to a wedge. Stand in a solid position over the stance foot. Use your poles to make sure balance is maintained.

Fig. b. Keep the stance leg stable with your balance completely over that foot. Begin to flatten the free foot to the snow and pull its heel toward the stance foot's heel.

Fig. c-d. As the free foot moves toward the stance foot, tip the ski toward the little toe edge. Feel that you're brushing the snow with the little toe edge. Ideally, only the ski edge touches the snow, while the entire ski base is facing the stance foot.

Fig. e. Now the skis are parallel and at the same angle to the snow. The skis must come to rest at the same angle.

a

b

Fig. 3-2. Stationary wedge to closure of free foot

c

Summary

After repeated practice, if you must make an adjustment to bring the skis to equal angles it indicates that an alignment check and correction is necessary. Once the skis reach a final position, place some weight on the free foot to create an evenly pressured stance. Alignment problems may appear early in the movements that we introduce. We believe that this is an extremely beneficial aspect of our program. If alignment problems are resolved early, you will progress more quickly.

Comfort and progress of the student dictate the pace and speed through these exercises. People who have backgrounds in sports like ice and in-line skating and dance may find the exercises easy to perform, and can move through them quickly. Other readers may find that they need practice time to refine the movements and become comfortable with balance on one foot. Find your own pace, and be confident you can perform each exercise before you move on. If you are taking ski instruction, express your comfort level; if the instructor is moving along too quickly, ask for more practice time.

Bullets
- Balance on the stance foot
- Draw the wedged free foot to parallel

3-3.   Sliding wedge to relaxed closure

The photos in this exercises may appear similar to all the others in this chapter to the first time observer. If you look more closely there are very important differences in ability levels demonstrated. Look for how soon the skis come to parallel as the exercises advance.

These basic movements in this exercise are the same as in the previous one, except you are moving forward as you perform them. The path of travel is less important than the distribution of balance. Here, you use the essence of the stance foot - free foot relationship.

In Brief

Start on the slope in a traversing position as in Chapter 2, exercise 2-7. Start sliding forward across the slope in a slightly downhill direction. As in the previous exercise, establish balance on the stance foot, then move the back of the free foot ski up the slope. The exercise may be started from a wedge. The forward motion will create some drag on the free (skier's left) ski. Use this drag to help pull the ski in toward the stance foot. As the free foot approaches the stance foot you may notice the stance ski changing direction slightly aiming uphill. The direction change will gradually slow you to a stop. Step the tips down to redirect the skis downhill and start the movements again.

d

e

Details

Fig. a-b. Getting to this position requires moving the tail of the free ski (the skier's left) up the slope while moving forward.

Fig. b. While moving with the skis in this "V" position, relax the muscles in the leg of the free foot and let the drag of the snow against the ski pull it toward the stance foot.

Fig. c-d. You can slow the rate of closure by continuing to push the free ski up the slope but preferably help to draw it closer by pulling the free foot heel toward the stance foot.

Fig. d-e. Once the skis are parallel continue the pulling and tipping movements with the free foot. Tip the free foot toward its little toe side.

*Fig. 3-3. Sliding wedge to phantom closure of free foot
(Shading indicates stance side)*

a

b

c

Fig. e. Pull the free boot right up against the stance foot. The actions of the free foot will direct the stance ski into the slope, creating a slight turn.

Summary

The stance ski should feel like it is brushing or spreading snow with some edge grip while turning. Make balance adjustments with the foot and ankle inside the boot. Try relaxing the stance foot and ankle; does that flatten the ski? Now tense it; notice how the stance ski reacts. Ideally you should travel across the snow at a forty-five degree angle to the hill. Raising the free foot will result in more edge grip of the stance ski adding more turning ability. Allowing the free foot to touch and brush over the snow as it draws toward the stance foot will create more turning arc, and is preferable. Experiment with both approaches. On a wide slope this sequence of opening and closing can be repeated many times in succession.

This exercise should require very little effort. Ski design will do all the work if you keep your body balanced over the stance foot. Soon you will combine the balancing ability and the movements of the free foot to ski parallel.

Bullets
- Balance on a moving stance foot
- Tip the free ski flat, and then to the little toe edge
- Draw the free ski toward the stance foot

Previous: *Sliding wedge to relaxed closure*

3-4.   **Wedge to Phantom Move**

Next: *Wedge to phantom closure, free foot lifted*

Phantom Move: turning your stance ski with the free foot

Now you can refine the movements you have already learned. This is the essence of the Primary Movements Teaching System. No task is too large because it is a logical step from the last movement. Now it is time to become more aggressive with the movements already in your repertoire. Lighten the free foot sooner in the descent and draw it toward the stance foot more quickly and aggressively. You can also try drawing the foot in with slight tapping or stepping actions. Lift the heel of the free ski and step it in to the stance foot in three separate movements. Set the free ski on its little toe edge each time it touches the snow. Strive for gentle tapping movements, not heavy-footed stomping.

The goal in this exercise is to start tipping the free foot sooner. The early lightening and tipping of the free foot is called the Phantom Move. The phantom move, when performed properly, is smooth, progressive, and barely detectable, hence its name. Notice how in this exercise, with the added emphasis on the phantom move, the skis are parallel by *fig. c.*

d

e

f

The last three photos, *fig. d-f*, emphasize the strong tipping of the free foot.

All this activity starts with the free foot. The kinetic chain moves up the body and through the pelvis over to the stance leg, producing the turning action of the stance ski. Movement and balance break down if the actions start higher in the body.

The results of muscular activity and ski performance are most effective if started at the foot level. Sensations from the foot tell us how the ski is behaving and how to adjust the foot. Consequently, focusing on the feet yields precise control.

Fig. 3-4. Wedge to strong phantom closure of free foot

In Brief
From a wedge, draw the free foot toward the stance foot for a parallel finish to this turn.

Details
Fig. a. Start in a wedge but balance on the stance foot. Move down and across the slope.

Fig. b. Tip the free foot over to its little toe edge as you glide the ski over the snow.

Fig. c. No time to be passive - keep coaxing the free foot over to its little toe edge and draw it closer. Tipping is easier as the feet get closer together.

Fig. d. Tip the free foot more aggressively to bring it farther onto edge than the stance foot.

Fig. e. Don't stop now! Keep your free foot light, pull the free heel toward the stance heel, and continue to tip the free foot. Watch the skis turn.

Fig. f. Remarkably, the skis are turning with virtually no effort or strength. This is the phantom move.

Summary

Notice how my belt buckle aligns vertically over the inside edge of my stance ski. This occurs while the free foot is still in a wedge. Emphasis on tipping has also yielded a free foot ski that is tipped uphill farther (*fig. d*) than the stance foot. Is the knee of my free leg pointed up the hill? Only as the result of actively tipping the free foot. Don't succumb to instructions that focus on knee movement. I have never felt my ski's edge with my knee. I can't keep track of so many body parts when I ski; it requires too much concentration. How can you control the whole body at once?

Keep it simple: "focus on your feet."

Let's discuss the role of the skis in this process. The new skis help tremendously in this system. Although I write about primary movements for shaped skis, I used them on and they are still effective for traditional skis. Shaped skis make it easier and quicker to learn. To experience immediate success with the Primary Movements Teaching System at low speeds, use shaped skis.

For readers who are fascinated by the technical perspective of skiing, note the lack of activity of the stance leg. The difference from other teaching methods is astounding. Traditional systems would have you focus entirely on turning, twisting, and steering the leg on the stance side of the body. Twisting disrupts balance, so focus on tipping the free foot to stay in balance. The Primary Movements Teaching System approach creates and reinforces balance.

Bullets

- Use the free foot to turn the stance ski

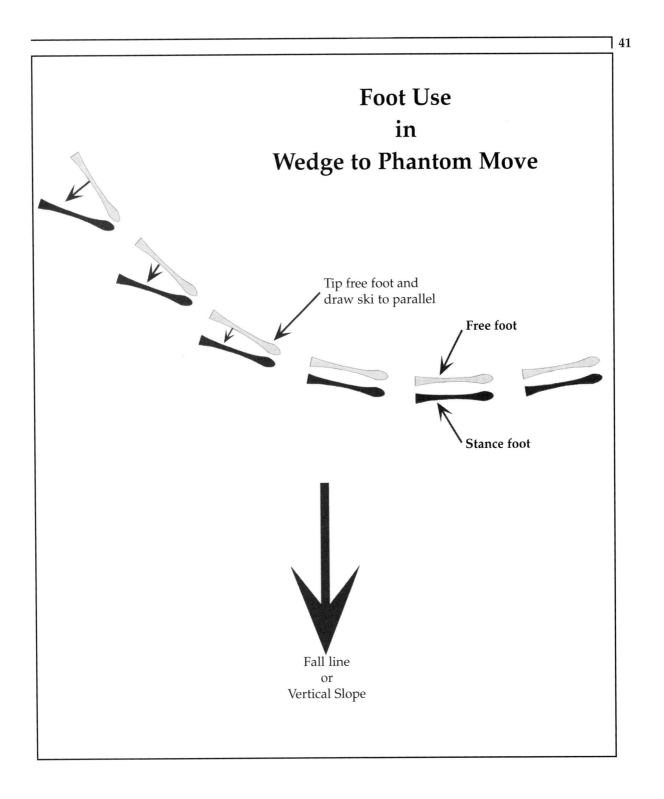

Foot Use
in
Wedge to Phantom Move

Tip free foot and
draw ski to parallel

Free foot

Stance foot

Fall line
or
Vertical Slope

Previous: *Wedge to phantom move*

3-5. **Wedge to phantom closure, free foot lifted**

Next: *Phantom move with ski on snow*

Fig. 3-5. Shallow wedge traverse to phantom move with free foot lifted   *c*

This exercise is deliberate and emphatic in edge use because it forces body shifts and deliberate balance changes. Use it to enhance stance foot edge grip. The exercise is rarely used today, although its roots are in the early Austrian systems. Aggressive ski lifting causes immediate edging in a dramatic fashion. Use this technique on aggressive terrain to engage the skis.

In Brief
Lift the tail of the free foot from the wedged, "V" position to transfer balance to the stance foot. Place the free foot parallel to the stance foot and tip the free foot to the little toe side (phantom move).

Details
Fig. a. Start across the hill in a narrow wedge, ready to pick up the free foot.
Fig. b. The tail of the free ski is raised; keep the tip on the snow for balance and guidance.
Fig. c. Set the free foot on the snow temporarily as you narrow the stance. Continue tipping and aggressively drawing the free ski in toward the stance foot.
Fig. d. Raise the tail of the free ski, keeping the tip on the snow, to tighten the arc. Pull the free foot close to the stance ski.
Fig. e. Finish the exercise balanced on the stance foot.

d

e

Summary

Stance width has a huge impact on your success at one-footed balance. Notice in *fig. a* and *b* how far the upper body leans out over the stance foot. When the feet are wide apart, a large movement of the upper body is required to be able to lift the free foot and stay in balance over the stance foot. See Fig. 12-5 & 12-6 in Chapter 12 for a comparison of balance with different stance widths. *Fig. a* displays how the body is preparing to balance solely over the stance foot. Even the stance width demonstrated in *fig. a* may cause difficulty establishing one-footed balance. However, when the free foot is drawn in close to the stance foot, the stance narrows, and balancing on one foot requires a less extreme body movement. Narrow your stance to make transferring movements smoother and to stay balanced.

Bullets

- Stand completely on the stance foot
- Draw the free foot aggressively to parallel

Previous: *Wedge to phantom closure, free foot lifted*

3-6.   **Phantom move with ski on snow**

Next: *Releasing movements*

Fig. 3-6. Wedge to phantom move sequence; free foot on snow

Now you are at the point where the exercises culminate to produce an instant phantom move. The phantom move is becoming increasingly important in the movement progression. You can already sense the power of its action. Phantom movements create control, and change turn radius. This exercise demonstrates how effortlessly you can break out of the wedge and become a permanently parallel skier. Balancing over the stance foot and using the free foot to engage the stance ski will cause the skis to arc across the snow. New shaped skis turn virtually by themselves using the phantom move. Don't hinder them by twisting the stance foot - notice how in all of the exercises in this chapter the stance leg remains stable and doesn't move. The phantom move of the free foot produces the desired actions. Most observers can't see the origins of actions in turns made by skiers using primary movements. If you watch expert skiers, it's difficult to describe how they turn so effortlessly. They have reduced their need for energy and effort by directing their turns with subtle foot movements like the phantom move.

In Brief
Change direction by tipping the free ski early in the turn. Narrow your stance as soon as possible, maintaining balance on the stance foot.

Details
Fig. a. Start moving across the slope, but more steeply into the fall line than in the previous exercises.

Fig. b. Start lightening your free foot. Keep the tip on the snow and lift the tail slightly. Flatten the free foot and start to draw it closer to the stance foot.

Fig. c. Once the skis are parallel and balance is totally over the stance foot, continue the tipping action. The free foot looks like it is on the snow, yet it is completely unweighted. Keep it close enough to the snow to feel the edge grazing the surface.

Fig. d-e. Engage the stance ski by the free foot tipping action. Maintain the arc by increased tipping action of the free foot.

Summary
Notice how the distance between the knees is constant from *fig. c* through *e.* This is a product of the free foot's tipping action; movements other than of the free foot would make the skis come apart. Practice free foot action to familiarize yourself with the little toe side of the foot and ski.

Notice the hand position. The consistent hand position in each frame demonstrates that no rotation was used in the legs, feet, or body to produce this turn. The stance leg had no role in the turn apart from balancing. The skis did the turning with some input from the free foot. The skis are actually carving a turn, even at these slow speeds. Resist the temptation to turn the feet or legs because turning attempts by the stance leg will eliminate carving and replace it with an unstable skid.

Bullets
• Bring the skis parallel and describe a turn using the Phantom Move

Angles of Descent
on the
Slope

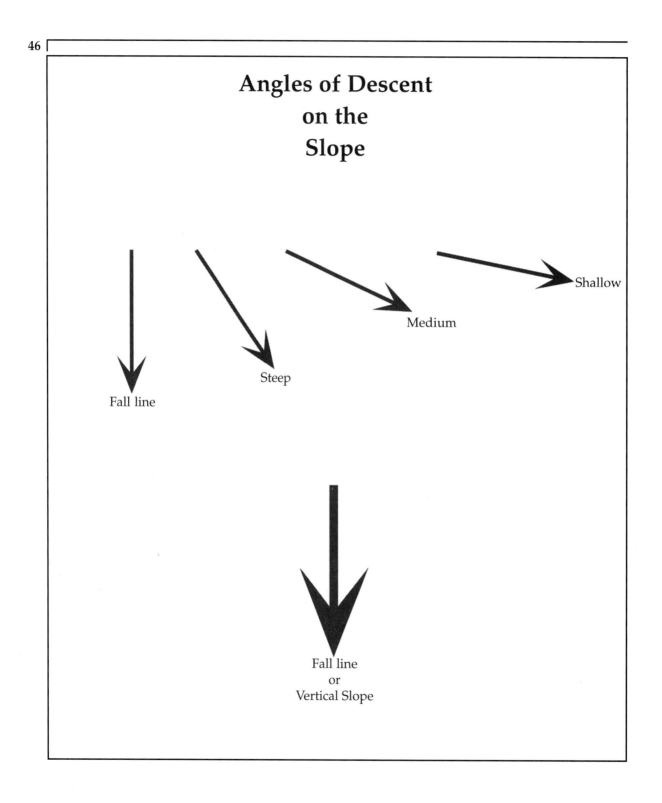

Fall line

Steep

Medium

Shallow

Fall line
or
Vertical Slope

Chapter 4 - Release

Releasing movements in the Primary Movements Teaching System are the actions that begin to **link parallel turns**. The last chapter taught how to get rid of the wedge. Now we have to make sure it doesn't creep back in at the beginning of a new turn. Most skiers have difficulty throughout their skiing careers eliminating wedge turn entries. The most likely point of ski tail flaring is in linked parallel turns between the exit of one turn and the entry of the next, the transition. The wedge entry produces a wedge Christie at best, which is not a great place to get stuck. Parallel skiing is a totally different experience; it introduces the true adventure of skiing.

Skillful releasing movements generated by foot actions are critical to breaking the wedge entry habit. In a parallel turn entry, the legs move simultaneously but each leg is performing different actions. Don't forget that simultaneous means at the same time; it doesn't mean in the same manner. The muscle activities that generate a release come from different muscles in each leg, working in different directions. Start the movements with the feet. The feet are connected to the ankles and boots, which in turn move the legs and so on up the body - the kinetic chain. These movements produce important skiing sensations that are felt on the bottom of the feet and are recorded by the brain. Although these movements have been traditionally taught by referring to the movement of the knees, the knees don't give clear sensations or accurate ski feedback. Your feet can perceive true skiing sensations. Since the feet are the primary movers, they have the ability to fine tune and control, so focus and begin all movements there. Simultaneous leg actions will happen more easily if the primary movers are at the base of the kinetic chain, the feet.

The introductory movements in the first chapters provide basic movement elements for this chapter. If you have been diligent about practicing the previous exercises, these new releasing movements will be easy. Releasing is the lateral movement started by the feet. By transferring pressure from one side of the boot to the other we effectively tip the skis. Effective foot movements have a positive balancing impact on the legs and upper body.

At first, identifying how to move your feet can take some concentration. Try these simple experiments. Sit on a chair with shoes or socks on. Do not look down at your feet. Attempt to react immediately to the following instructions. Roll your left foot to its little toe side. Now roll your right foot to its big toe side. Don't peek - use the sensations from the soles of your feet to confirm that the feet have tipped in the same direction. Notice the actions of the legs (kinetic chain) as a result of the foot movements. This foot tipping exercise demonstrates that foot movements control leg movements. If you learn to perform the same movements on-snow, in boots, you will get both skis to release at the same time and maintain a parallel position. Now let's apply it to the skiing exercises.

Fall line

The term fall line will be used throughout the book. The fall line is the steepest line heading down the slope. Gravity's greatest pull is straight down the fall line. Gravity, of course, is constant, but the steeper the hill, the more gravity pulls you down the slope.

Movement progression continues on following page

4-1.   Release to sideslip

Releasing movements are tied closely to the sideslip. The sideslip has been a part of ski teaching for at least fifty years. It has been used to teach skiers how to use their edges. In this case, the exercise is an introduction to movements that will begin turns. The first time side slipper should try progressive tipping movements of the feet toward the slope before full releases are attempted. Sense the edges of the skis against the snow as they roll from edged and gripping to flat and slippery. Once the skis flatten to the point where they can slip, the fun begins.

In Brief

Practice tipping back and forth from a static stance before attempting a complete flattening of the skis that initiates motion. Flatten your skis by a progressive, lateral foot movement. The flattening movement will start the skis and their tips moving vertically down the slope. Continue to roll, tip, or tilt the ankles and feet to flatten the skis.

Details

Fig. a. With feet equally weighted, start to roll the stance foot (skier's left) flat toward the little toe. Slowly follow with the free foot but let it lag a fraction behind. Just before you start to slip sideways, roll both feet back onto their edges. Repeat this until you get the feel for controlling the lateral movements of the feet.

Fig. b. Now make one continuous, progressive movement to flatten both skis to the snow. Flatten the stance foot slightly ahead of the free foot. Allow the skis to move a few feet at a time before reengaging the edges. Reposition the skis for another comfortable start.

Summary

Feel the transition from gripping to slipping by the ski-snow interaction. This will give you a smooth and balanced release. Abrupt body movements cause the skis to react unexpectedly, putting you beyond your realm of experience. The bottom line is, don't surprise your skis.

Keep the edging angles of the skis steady once you start moving. The ski tips may drop down the slope relative to the starting position as you flatten the skis, which is desirable. The dropping of the tips may cause you to move forward across the slope. When the skis do start to slip and move forward, continue with the movement. Be patient and use the phantom move learned in the previous chapter to slow and turn back into and up the slope.

Bullets

- Flatten both feet to release
- Roll the skis on and off an edged stance
- Allow the skis to move with the releasing action

Fig. 4-1. Release to sideslip

Previous: *Release to sideslip*

4-2.   Full release on green terrain

Next: *Full release on green*

a   *b*

Fig. 4-2. Full release on green terrain

This exercise is the next logical step in refining the foot flattening activities needed to ski parallel. Your ability and comfort with this movement determines your preparedness for a parallel turn. The exercises in the release chapter develop the upper third of the turn, each step bringing you closer to the full release into the next turn. The advanced release maneuver includes a balance and stance foot change, unlocking the parallel connection from one turn to the next.

In Brief

Release as you did in the previous exercise, but as the skis start moving forward and down the slope, allow the flattening motion to move you forward at least five feet before you reengage or tip the skis. Resume the flattening movements, combining forward motion and flattening. Use the phantom move to bring the skis back into the slope to slow and stop.

Details

Fig. a. Stand across the slope evenly balanced on both feet. Keep your hands forward and to the side to maintain a stable upper body.

c   d

Fig. b. Start to flatten both feet making sure the stance foot leads the actions. Lighten the stance foot slightly to flatten it. Flatten it by tilting it toward the little toe side. Continue flattening until both feet make the skis slip down the slope.

Fig. c. Let the skis float over the snow, maintaining a consistent position with your feet.

Fig. d. At the point when you are headed down the slope, start to tip your skis back onto their edges by using the phantom move. Lighten and tip the free foot (skier's right) toward the little toe edge to head back up and into the slope to slow and stop.

Summary

The skis will feel slippery and a little out of control just before you move with them. Moving skis are best controlled by fine lateral movements of the ankles and feet.

The skis should move together, even though the stance foot starts the release to the little toe edge slightly before the free foot. Releasing the stance foot involves taking the pressure off the big toe side and transferring it to the little toe side. Lighten the stance foot as you make this transfer. Further on in the exercises you will be lifting the stance foot at this moment. Clearing it from the snow saves you from catching the edge and tumbling over it.

Keep your body over the skis as you start moving with them. Maintain slightly flexed ankles and knees to remain centered on your skis. Feel your shins in contact with the front of the boot, but avoid leaning on the front of the boot for support.

If you have constant problems with the free foot edge hooking on its big toe side when you flatten your skis, flatten it less or stop flattening that foot. For knock-kneed skiers, this is a common occurrence. People with bowed legs find that it is easy to flatten the stance leg. The bowlegged skier's stance leg is naturally flat to the snow, so it requires strong adduction (pressing the stance knee in toward the slope) to keep it edged. Bowlegged skiers often complain that their knees hurt because they must force the knee into the slope to get on an edge. Notice, for the first time I referred to muscles high on the leg (adductors) to create movement. This is the traditional way to think about movement. Many of the situations and difficulties that present themselves in skiing are a result of misalignment. Without proper alignment, the instructor has no choice but to use adaptive approaches. Almost all skiers, if misaligned, learn adaptive skiing. If alignment training is provided and biomechanically based teaching systems are used, adaptive movements will be eliminated from skiing.

Bullets
- Flatten both skis with the stance foot leading slightly
- Once the skis start to slide, keep them at that edging angle
- Use the phantom move to head the skis back up the hill

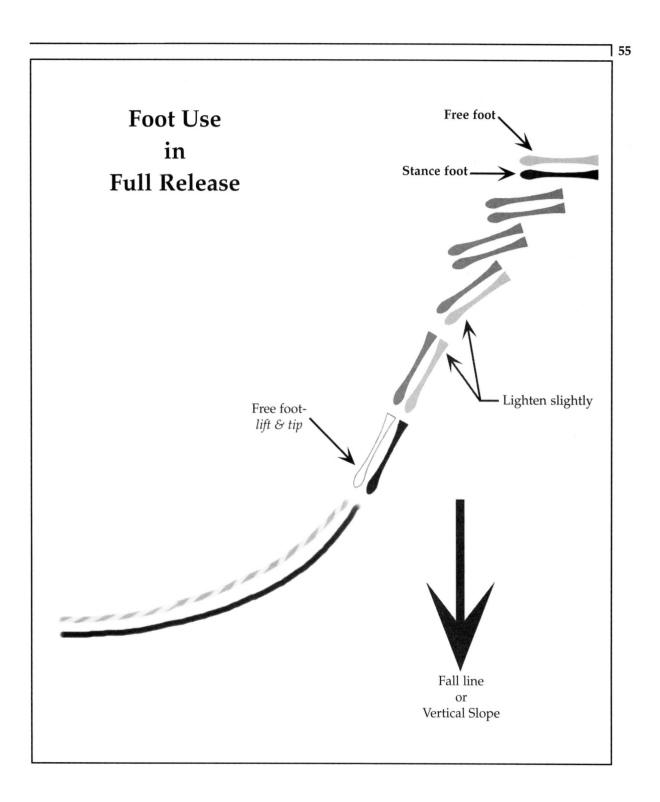

Foot Use
in
Full Release

Free foot

Stance foot

Lighten slightly

Free foot-
lift & tip

Fall line
or
Vertical Slope

Previous: *Full release on green terrain*
4-3. Full release on green
Next: *Full release on blue terrain*

Fig. 4-3. Full release on green terrain

The actions that change ski direction start at the feet. The feet tip to flatten the skis, the legs react to ski tilt angle, and the body reacts to the legs moving beneath it. This is the kinetic chain at work.

In Brief

This series of photos demonstrates how the skis change direction from an across slope to down slope position. The movements that drive this direction change are similar to the ones in previous exercises. Keep the skis working in unison laterally, as if your boots were on a monoski or a snowboard. Tip the feet as if movement of one foot made the other foot move.

Details

Fig. a. Start in a comfortable, stable position.

Fig. b. Start the flattening movements of the feet slowly; prepare to stand over the skis as they begin to slip.

Fig. c. Flattening the feet moves the legs away down the slope.

Fig. d. Loose, relaxed ankles allow the skis to float and turn over the snow.

Fig. e. Just as the ski tips head into the slope, lighten the stance foot and tip it to the little toe side.

Fig. f. Pick up the stance foot if you are ready to go to the next turn. If you are unsure of your balance, bring the skis back up the slope onto their edges using the phantom move.

d

e

f

Summary

Relaxed ankles are facilitated by proper boot fit and foot beds that allow for co-contraction. (Read about co-contraction in the alignment section, Chapter 12). From the view in the photo series, it is apparent that I am well aligned. The space between my legs remains constant through the whole exercise. The skis stay at the same angle to the snow. At every point of movement and for every exercise in this chapter, a student's equipment is evaluated to make sure it is not impeding progress. Improper boots, boot fit, or foot beds can seriously reduce your ability to make progressive and simultaneous releasing movements.

Bullets
- Move progressively to flatten the skis
- Practice balance transfers by lightening the tail of the stance ski

Previous: *Full release on green*

4-4.   Full release on blue terrain

Next: *Full release on blue*

a

b

Fig. 4-4. Full release on blue terrain   *c*

You may find it easier to release on steeper terrain because gravity has more pull on the skis to start them slipping. On the steeper slope you will also be able to keep the skis at higher (steeper) edge angles, while still moving and slipping down the hill. Notice in this series of photos how the commitment to the release movement is more aggressive: the skis already point down the slope by *fig. d*. As you practice and become comfortable with the releasing movements, floating the skis over the snow with balance and control will seem easy and reassuring.

In Brief

Flatten the feet to bring the ski tips down the slope. Practice balance transfers by lightening the stance foot as you get your tips to a steeper angle on the slope.

Details

Fig. a. Start in a comfortable, stable position.

Fig. b. Start the flattening movements of the feet slowly; prepare to stay with the skis as they begin to slip.

Fig. c. Lighten the back of the stance ski once that ski has flattened. Continue to move the skis while maintaining the same edge angles to the snow.

Fig. d. Tip the lightened stance leg to its little toe edge to help turn the uphill ski down the slope.

Fig. e. Decide to continue lightening the stance foot until it is free from the snow or to place it back on the snow. If you decide to continue the release and transition to the new direction, commit to a complete balance transfer. Once you have transferred and are standing on the uphill ski (new stance foot, skier's right) tip the free foot further to bring the stance ski through the turn. To pull out of the steep angle to the slope and avoid entering the new turn, lift the uphill free foot and tip it to the little toe side.

d

e

Watch For

Foot movement generates ankle control. Although the foot doesn't actually move very much in a well fitting ski boot, the movements of the foot articulate the ankle and apply pressure to the side of the boot as the ankle bone pushes against the liner. This articulation tips the boot. When the ankle is floating, it doesn't apply pressure to either side of the boot. Stance is centered over the foot, with the foot comfortable and relaxed. When the ankle floats, you sense a flat ski on the snow. The shaped skis make tipping actions easier to control because of their width at the tip and tail. The skis reduce over-edging, making the skis less reactive to slight miscues in tipping. They give the learning skier more time to recover when inconsistent or inadvertent foot movements are made.

Bullets
• Lift the tail of the stance foot to practice a complete balance transfer

4-5. Full release on blue

Next: *Garland with wedge*

Fig. 4-5. Full release on blue terrain

Use of the upper body isn't required to flatten the skis and change their direction. The upper body change that is demonstrated here is a result of the flattening actions started at the feet.

Details

Fig. a-e. A series of smooth, progressive, flattening actions of both skis brings the tips down and slightly forward. Flatten the stance foot by tipping it toward the little toe side of the ski. The free foot follows through a simultaneous effort by lowering the big toe edge of its ski.

Summary

In many cases, learning skiers are fearful of flattening the skis because the accompanying sensations are of slipperiness and lack of control. If I were launched for the first time onto a pond in a kayak, fear would be my first feeling as well. Although I have never been in a kayak, I imagine that once you start tipping and rolling, it must be difficult to stop. Kayaks don't have edges. Skiers can feel in control when stationary on skis because our edges are firmly engaged in the snow. Unlike the kayak, though, side or forward slipping on skis still provides easy access to the edges. With practice, releasing and reengaging the edges will become a familiar movement.

It is difficult to maneuver skis at slow speed if the edges are dug in. At higher speeds, later on, progressive edge angle increases are mandatory for control of carving skis. At slow speeds, the flatter the ski is to the snow, the easier it is to change direction, especially on a shaped ski. Control can be achieved quickly with correct and efficient movements. Subtle movements such as lightening or tipping a foot can change the dynamics of the ski. These skis need very little input to create wonderful actions. But what does subtle mean? If you try any of these movements and the reactions of the skis surprise you or scare you, the movements weren't subtle enough. Like pouring fine wine, make slow movements to flow the liquid without splashing it; be patient with the slow filling of the glass and enjoy the moment.

Bullets

- Use foot flattening and engaging movements to refine lateral movement

This exercise combines all the basic elements of the turn at an introductory level. It can be done with the beginning stepping movements as described in Chapter 2, exercises 7 and 8, or by using releasing movements as introduced in this chapter. This series of photos demonstrates movements that still require some refining. The example will illustrate how to reinforce the correct movements while detecting movements that are counterproductive and might interfere with progress.

The skier who has used stepping and releasing movements as an introduction to skiing is on a direct parallel path. The direct parallel skier takes complete advantage of the new shaped ski design and of the biomechanical accuracy of this system. This approach and experience pays off greatly at this level of skiing. Continued work toward accurate foot tipping and lifting actions will imprint the movements that take you beyond this series to the advanced and expert skier levels.

The ability to transfer balance as introduced in the phantom move is given renewed emphasis in these exercises. Connected turns require free foot actions right from the beginning of the turn. Focus on the phantom move to refine this garland exercise. The garland gives you the ability to ski down the mountain connecting the movements learned in Chapters 2 through 4. Garlands also give the sensation of real skiing. The garland demonstrated here comes close to actual turns on a slope. You are not learning new movements, rather assembling those you have already practiced. Nonstop skiing refinement and important practice miles can be achieved with garlands. Garlands can also be used to negotiate more intimidating slopes, avoiding the direct route down the fall line. I use garlands to teach almost all movements, including those for bump skiing.

In Brief

Release until the tips head down the slope. Use the phantom move to bring the skis back into the slope.

Details

Fig. a. Start the releasing movements by flattening the feet to the snow surface.

Fig. b. Continue to flatten the skis as they start turning toward the fall line. Lagging release of the stance foot (skier's left) has caused the stance ski to point slightly toward the free ski, forming a "V". Flattening the free foot too actively also contributes to the wedge. To keep the skis parallel, lighten and tip the stance foot to the little toe side more aggressively.

Fig. c. The skis have turned far enough to start the turn back into the slope. Notice there is still a pronounced wedge. The demonstrator has omitted the balance transfer to the new (skier's right) stance foot between *fig. c* and *d*. The position of the skis reveals a skier who is not ready to go directly to parallel and who is stuck between turns. I illustrate this here to bring up the different movements that limit development. Tipping the uphill, free foot to its big toe edge too quickly or failing to lighten and tip the stance ski sufficiently toward its little toe edge generates the wedge. The skier is still trying to turn left (skier's left), but rather than using the phantom move of the left

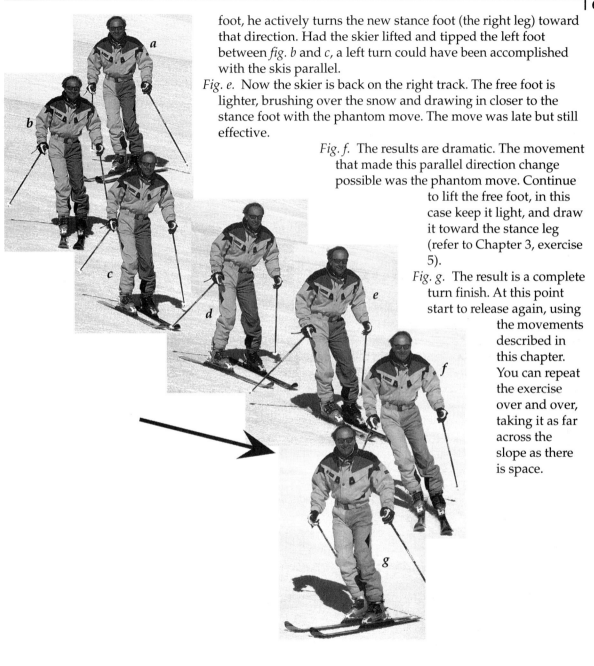

foot, he actively turns the new stance foot (the right leg) toward that direction. Had the skier lifted and tipped the left foot between *fig. b* and *c*, a left turn could have been accomplished with the skis parallel.

Fig. e. Now the skier is back on the right track. The free foot is lighter, brushing over the snow and drawing in closer to the stance foot with the phantom move. The move was late but still effective.

Fig. f. The results are dramatic. The movement that made this parallel direction change possible was the phantom move. Continue to lift the free foot, in this case keep it light, and draw it toward the stance leg (refer to Chapter 3, exercise 5).

Fig. g. The result is a complete turn finish. At this point start to release again, using the movements described in this chapter. You can repeat the exercise over and over, taking it as far across the slope as there is space.

Fig. 4-6. Garland with wedge

Summary

We find many skiers stuck in the situation between *fig. b* and *d*. The garland exercise demonstrated here is valuable for a number of reasons: the exercise allows practice of all the essential or primary movements of a complete turn; you may drop the tips down into the slope as far as you wish before returning to the phantom move; and, you can practice a gradual approach to the slope or venture a complete turn when you are confident with the movements.

The garland also breaks the turn into easy-to-practice components. The release is the beginning (in this example) of a turn to the left but when the turn nears the fall line you can pull away to complete a turn to the right.

All the exercises should be done in both directions. The focus for the exercise is gradually to head the skis directly down the slope before turning back into the slope. In *fig. c*, for example, try to continue flattening before coming back to the right.

The important movement omitted by the demonstrator is now obvious: it was the balance transfer. In *fig. b-d*, make a complete transfer to the stance foot. Select specific terrain for this exercise. A long traverse with a side slope is an excellent place to practice garlands. Often, cat tracks have perfect uphill banks from which to practice releases.

Bullets
- Transfer balance by lightening the stance foot
- Tip the free foot to change direction
- Transfer again by replacing the free foot
- Pick up the stance foot and lighten it to complete the garland

Chapter 5 - The Parallel Phantom Move

The Phantom Move is the precursor to the Phantom Turn, which is the backbone of the Primary Movements Teaching System. A phantom turn is connected phantom moves. When you can connect turns with phantom moves you will be an accomplished skier. The turn matures from humble movements learned at the first stages of the Primary Movements Teaching System. The phantom turn is used at the highest level of skiing by elite skiers. You can continue to develop and apply this turn to all disciplines and developments in skiing including bumps, powder, crud, ice, carving, and racing. The movements, because they are biomechanically based, will be applicable to any ski equipment innovation of the future.

Most sports that have a history of being studied intensely, like gymnastics, tennis, golf, baseball, and the martial arts, have fundamental movements; these fundamentals are refined so you become proficient in the sport. Learning a sport that requires a new set of movements at every stage of development makes the activity tedious and unrewarding. There is great waste in such a system as people often get stuck in dead-end patterns that are difficult to unlearn. So let's get it right from the beginning and do away with the rest. Learning primary movements requires diligence and dedication, as does any worthy endeavor, but while it is being perfected the building blocks remain a consistent foundation.

The ease and success of your experience validate the strength and accuracy of the system. As you progress in learning the primary movements, your ability to understand it and coach yourself will become evident. The movement cues will strengthen your skiing actions and sensations. Using these cues helps make the movements become natural, subconscious, and second nature. Because they are your formula for success, you become self-coached, discarding the need to have someone constantly looking over your shoulder to judge your performance. You develop your own intuition about right and wrong ways to move based on your feelings of balance, not on someone's opinions. This fosters a great sense of accomplishment.

The phantom move divides the body into logical performance sectors. The downhill side of the body (leg, ski, and foot) is responsible for creating a balance point; it is the stance side. The uphill side of the body is responsible for tipping actions; it is the free side. With this understanding we can determine and describe actions in a comprehensible way. For the reader and skiing enthusiast, having a clear understanding of which leg or foot is creating action at what point in a turn simplifies learning.

The exercises in this section refine movement ability and increase the demands on the skier by approaching the slope more directly. The exercises also put more emphasis on the proficiency of individual foot use. The last refinement of ability comes in progressing out of a finely skidded, lesser edge engagement turn to a higher degree of ski engagement in a carved turn.

Previous: *Garland with wedge*

5-1.   Forward sideslip to phantom move

Next: *Shallow traverse to phantom move*

The goal is to perform the phantom move, starting with skis parallel, and maintaining parallel skis through the release. The focus is on establishing a clean carving lower arc of the turn. We are building on the movements of the previous chapter where the focus was the upper third of the turn.

In Brief

Flatten both skis to get them moving forward and slightly down the slope. Keep the skis at a shallow angle to the slope; use the guiding ability of the free foot to change the direction of the stance foot and ski toward and into the slope. The bottom half of the arc in the snow is shaped like a crescent moon.

e

f

g

Details

Fig. a. Start with the skis pointed down at a shallow angle to the slope. Start moving forward in a traverse. Flatten and release the skis as you move forward. Open your feet slightly to create more space between the skis at the beginning of the movement, thus allowing for more room to draw in the free foot.

Fig. b. As you slowly begin tipping it onto the little toe side, draw the free foot (skier's left) over toward the stance foot (skier's right). This action will direct the stance ski gradually into the slope.

Fig. c & d. The skis are continuing a skidded forward slip, at a slow, progressive rate, developing into a skidded arc.

Fig. 5-1. Forward sideslip to strong phantom move with free foot

Fig. e-g. Increased tipping activity of the free foot causes the stance foot to tip to a higher angle, finish the arc, and come to a stop. Keep the angle of the stance foot similar to the free foot, initiating most of the adjustments with the free foot.

Summary

Drawing the free foot closer will begin the turning action of the stance ski. The exercise becomes a play between the snow and the skis. Your body and its movements are the instruments of control. Let the natural forces of gravity and friction do the work for you. Very little effort is required for this exercise. You will become the master of your environment if you practice patience and develop the small movements at the base of the body needed to control the shaped skis. In order to become proficient, repeat these movements across the whole slope. Cross the slope when it is not crowded.

Bullets
- Release the edges as you move forward
- Perform the phantom move

Previous: *Forward sideslip to phantom move*

5-2. Shallow traverse to phantom move

Next: *Aggressive phantom move*

In Brief

Adding dynamism to the first exercise can bring you to an earlier carving and engagement of the edge. All of the movements we have learned can be used on any terrain at any speed. Additional speed and steepness require more weight on and edge angle of the stance leg. The game is interesting because with more balance and pressure added to a higher edge angle you gain increased control and ski performance. This is easy to say, but it takes practice to feel comfortable with this tremendous ability.

When I learned to snowboard I knew that the board would work for me if I went faster and got it to a higher edge angle. This is great information and I thought about it every time I planted my tailbone in the snow. I started increasing edge angle too aggressively and abruptly; the board really caught the edge and started a very quick change of direction or turn. I wasn't ready for that much carving in such a short distance. I hadn't developed the ability to keep my body balanced over my feet. Carving produces the feeling that the board or ski picks up speed. In actuality, the ski isn't going faster, but it is relative to previous experience of moving with it and anticipating its actions. In learning carving, skiers have some advantages over the learning snowboarder. The boarder has only one base of support and must commit the whole board to edging; the consequences are abrupt, you are either on or off it. The skier has the stance foot as a base of support and can use the free foot to initiate and modulate the edging. By the time the stance ski reacts, a skier has time to adjust and, if necessary, detune the amount of edging and pressure.

(Continues on following page)

Details

Fig. a. From a forty-five degree angle to the slope, start moving forward in a traverse or forward sideslip.

Fig. b. Raise the tail of the free (left) foot from the snow.

Fig. c. Tip the free foot toward the little toe edge, tipping the entire ski; keep the ski raised (Phantom Move).

Fig. d. Keep the free ski tip on the snow while tipping and drawing the free foot closer to the stance foot.

Fig. e. Press the heel of the free foot against the stance foot while tipping it.

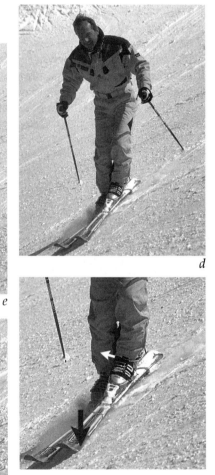

Fig. f. Reduce the amount of tipping as the skis slowly come to a stop.

Fig. 5-2. Phantom move from 45 degree angle to fall line

Summary

Continue to reinforce the movements generated by the foot and ankle. Balance is easy to maintain because the stance side of the body is stable and the stance ski is connected to and engaged in the snow while moving. Now you are carving.

Bullets
- Traverse on the stance foot
- Lift and tip the free foot
- Press the free foot against the stance foot

Previous: *Shallow traverse to phantom move*

5-3. Aggressive phantom move

Next: *Steep traverse to phantom move*

a

b

Fig. 5-3. Parallel traverse to phantom move with lifted free foot

From this different viewing angle, the actions of the free foot are evidenced by the lifting and spacing changes between the boots and knees. Balance is easily maintained in this maneuver if the raised, free foot is pulled in close to the stance foot. A wide stance with feet apart will eliminate the turning control of the free foot. A wide stance moves the center of balance too far into the slope, compromising balancing and carving. With emphasis on developing a proper kinetic chain, the raised foot action is designed to produce a positive ski engagement. The stability of the ankle of the stance foot can sometimes be the crucial element of one-foot balancing. Experiment with stabilizing the ankle by letting it relax or float; if wobble results, a proper foot bed and alignment may be needed. The exercise of relaxing the ankle can be a fine tuning element in your ski edging. It will definitely increase your understanding and feeling of engaged ski performance.

In Brief

Starting from a shallow traverse, pick up and slide the free foot to touch the stance boot. Pull the free boot up and tip it to its little toe edge as you press it against the stance boot.

Details

Fig. a. Start with skis sliding forward in a traverse.

Fig. b. Immediately raise the free foot and bring it in contact with the stance foot.

Fig. c. Touch the free boot to, and slide it along, the stance boot while raising it. Keeping the ski tip on the snow, tip the free foot toward the little toe side.

Fig. d. The belly of the turn is being completed with the actions started in *fig. a-c.*

c

d

Summary

Notice how pressing the free foot toward the stance foot has produced symmetry in leg angles to the snow. The muscles contracting to produce these positions and actions result in a powerful position of balance.

Raising the back of the free ski while the tip stays on the snow offers great performance benefits. The snow contact of the tip helps to engage the little toe side of the free ski, thus turning the skis. Tip contact focuses added turning power on the raised, free ski. This effect can be adjusted by the amount of pressure exerted on the tip.

Bullets
- Raise and tip the free foot while pressing it to the stance boot

Previous: *Aggressive phantom move*

5-4.   **Steep traverse to phantom move**

Next: *Fall line to phantom move*

a   *b*   *c*

Fig. 5-4. Steep parallel traverse to phantom move with free foot lifted

A more direct approach to the slope, almost straight into it, requires a longer arc and a longer balancing act. Movements that create the completion of the arc are started immediately and are exaggerated to develop confidence in the skis' action and ability to turn. The goal is to start the phantom movement by the free foot early in the descent, right after you start sliding. Repeat this exercise, increasing the steepness of descent at the start. You'll gain confidence that the phantom move will pull you into a turn up the hill.

In Brief

The movements are the same as in the previous exercise. Start at a steeper angle to the slope.

Details

Fig. a. Let the skis go toward the fall line.

Fig. b. Raise the free foot and start tipping it - the phantom move.

Fig. c. The stance foot is firmly engaged and the free foot raised to produce a balanced position.

Fig. d. Continue aggressive tipping movements to make the stance ski react.

Fig. e. Weight and balance over the stance leg has created the arc.

Fig. f. Be patient, bring the turn all the way back up into the slope for a stop. Put the free foot back on the snow as you stop.

Summary

As the free foot starts tipping, the stance ski will react by cutting into the snow. Keep the tail of the free foot raised slightly. Starting directly in the slope, raising the free foot and tipping it even slightly will bring the stance ski into a turn. Try this directly in the fall line on very flat terrain. Flat terrain also provides the opportunity to test your one-footed balance without intimidation. We test skier balance on one foot as part of a full alignment evaluation. Only the very poorly aligned skier is unable to stand on one foot and balance for a short run. One-footed balance improves almost immediately with a little practice. Proper alignment will make a tremendous difference in one-footed balancing exercises.

d

e

f

Bullets

• Pick up and tip the free foot immediately after starting down

Starting in the fall line requires the ability to stand on one foot at the start. It can be done on all ranges of slope steepness. It is demonstrated on blue terrain, but can easily be done on green. This is the advanced version, with a high degree of commitment demonstrated in the tipping and lifting action. The free foot is raised and the big toe edge of that foot and ski are brought into contact with the stance boot. Immediately raising the free foot and touching the inside ski edge to the stance boot creates aggressive tipping of the free foot. Try this in your living room: pick up the left foot and immediately touch the arch of that foot to the anklebone of your right foot. Notice how the little toe of the left foot tips down toward the floor; the same action occurs when you do this with skis.

In Brief

Starting directly in the fall line, lift the free foot and tip it aggressively. Bring the edge of the lifted ski in contact with the stance boot. Hold this position as the stance ski completes a turn back into the slope.

Details

Fig. a. Let the skis slide straight down the slope.

Fig. b. Raise the back of the free ski (left).

Fig. c. Tip the free ski and watch the stance ski react to the actions of the free foot. Make these movements immediately and deliberately.

c

d

Fig. 5-5. Phantom move with lifted free foot, starting in fall line

a

b

Fig. d. Continue to tip and lift the free foot; the stance ski will do the rest. Completion and turn size depends on how far you tip the free ski.

Summary

Remember, applying the primary movements works simply and logically in every sense: for example, pick up and tip the right ski to turn right; pick up and tip the left foot to go left. This holds true throughout the system.

The amount and size of turn depends on these three elements:

1. Balance on the stance ski
2. Amount of tipping
3. Shape or side cut of the ski.

The turn will start more quickly, or hook faster, if you stand more forward on the skis or in your boots. You can accomplish this by raising the back of the free ski while keeping its tip on the snow. This action brings your stance slightly more forward. Putting the ski tail back on the snow moves your body slightly more rearward.

Now you're ready to connect phantom movements, so we'll proceed with some garlands.

Bullets

- Start straight down the slope
- Immediately balance on one ski

5-6.   Parallel garland with free foot lifted

Garlands appeared in previous chapters: stepping in Exercise 2-8, and with a wedge in Exercise 4-6. Now use the garland for parallel turn practice. The first of two exercises uses the lifted tail of the free ski and the Phantom Move. The second is similar, but with the refinement of keeping the free ski on the snow.

Use the parallel releasing movements from Chapter 4 and the phantom move from this chapter and you've got the makings of parallel garlands. This exercise is perfect for a solid taste of parallel skiing movements. Since you have already learned all the components of this exercise it is a matter of combining and merging them in the right order. The play of foot movements begins. Take lots of runs and learn to connect the phantom moves.

In Brief

From a stationary, comfortable stance across the slope, release the skis and direct them to the fall line (the arrow in fig 5-6 indicates the vertical slope). Lift the free ski tail and use the phantom move to bring the skis back up the slope. Before you come to a stop, release the skis to repeat the exercise.

Details

Fig. a. Choose a slope that is comfortable to negotiate but steep enough for gravity to assist in ski use. Release both skis to keep them parallel.

Fig. b. Continue to flatten both skis and begin to lighten the free foot (skier's left).

Fig. c. As the skis turn almost directly down the slope, reverse the actions of lightening by lifting the right free foot to bring the skis back to the right into the slope.

Fig. d. Press the free foot (skier's right) firmly against the stance boot and tip it toward its little toe.

Fig. e. Press your knees together and tip the free foot to the little toe side. Move the stance leg to maintain contact with the free leg, matching its movements and position.

Fig. f. Complete the turn by continued free foot lightening and tipping. Now it is time to start the next release to go back down the slope. Ski in an uninterrupted garland by placing the free foot back on the snow, flattening the skis, then using the phantom move.

Summary

Garlands are the best way to combine practice and skiing. Pick a slope that is not crowded and look uphill before starting. Avoid skier traffic. The garland can become a game of "chicken" with the vertical slope. When you prolong the release and use the phantom move in the releasing direction you may end up going straight down the slope. Then, if you continue to increase the lightening and tipping of the left foot you will come to a completed turn to the left. However, the idea of the garland is to practice the bottom of the arc by repeating the movements as you cross the slope. Therefore, before you are heading directly down the slope, stand and balance back on the left ski and use the phantom move of the right foot to bring the arc back to your starting direction. Perform all these exercises in both directions.

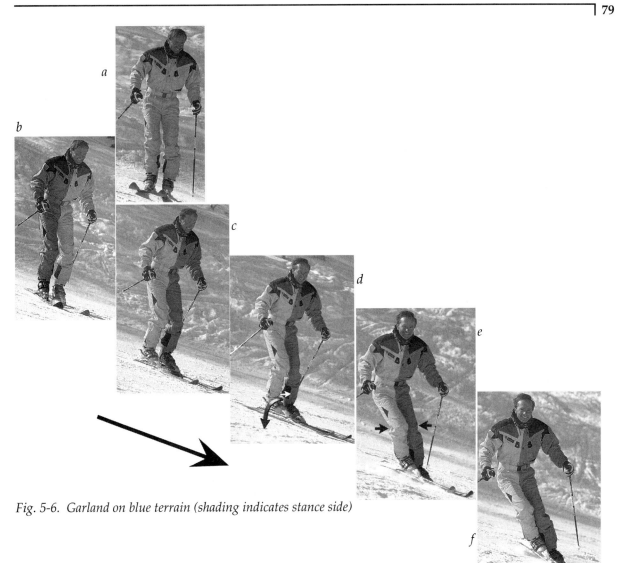

Fig. 5-6. Garland on blue terrain (shading indicates stance side)

Bullets
- Release to the fall line
- Lift the free ski tail and use the phantom move to come back to the starting direction
- Repeat the sequence

Previous: *Parallel garland with free foot lifted*

5-7. Parallel garland, free foot on snow

Next: *The complete turn*

Your ability to ski with refined parallel movements depends on balance on the stance ski. Movements of the free foot direct turning and ski control. Most skiers never appreciate this level of balancing ability and thus never sense carving by the stance ski.

Initially, to learn one-footed balance it is important to keep the free foot raised; this means you are balancing at the required level. If you place the free foot inadvertently on the snow it indicates a loss of lateral balance. It is important to your skiing development that balancing be exercised with this rigor. Skiing proficiency is lost when one-foot balancing is compromised. Once you feel and understand what balance is, you will know when you lose it. You have learned the art of balance and you should be in tune with it in every ski turn.

It is possible that your sense of balance is much more acute since learning primary movements. You are ready to refine your skiing by gradually placing the free foot on the snow. Balance sensitivity will allow you to maintain contact of the free foot with the snow and still use it as the primary tuner of turns. When the free foot is on the snow it performs exactly as it did when lifted. For the purpose of this exercise, the free foot skims the surface without being pressured. Turn the stance ski by using the phantom move with the free foot skimming over the snow.

In Brief

From a stationary, comfortable stance across the slope, release the skis and direct them to the fall line. Keeping the free ski brushing the snow, use the phantom move to bring the skis back into the slope. Before you come to a stop, release the skis to repeat the exercise.

Details

Fig. a. Start from a comfortable stance on an easy slope. Release both skis.

Fig. b. Continue to flatten the skis but start to lighten the free foot (skier's left) as if you were turning left. Keep the free foot (left) brushing the snow while you tip it.

Fig. c. As you approach the direct line down the slope, stop tipping and shift balance to stand on that foot by lightening the new free foot (skier's right). Tip the right foot to turn to the right up the slope.

Fig. d. Balance on the stance foot (left) and tip the free foot further toward its little toe side. As the stance ski starts to turn up the hill, keep the free foot equidistant from the stance foot. Feel the little toe edge of the free foot gently brushing on the snow.

Fig. e. The free foot tips further toward the little toe edge, causing the stance ski to turn up the hill. To move into the next garland, wait to slow sufficiently then release both skis.

Summary

The challenge in this exercise is keeping the free foot at the same distance from the stance foot throughout the turn. This exercise develops important new sensations through refined, smaller movements. The tipping movement of the free foot inside the ski boot makes fine tuning possible.

Success may not be achieved the first time out, but bear with the effort required. Your balance transfers will become more subtle, making turn connecting easier. Err on the side of keeping the free foot off the snow rather than standing on both feet equally.

Bullets
- Lighten and tip rather than lifting the free ski from the snow
- Brush the snow with the free foot

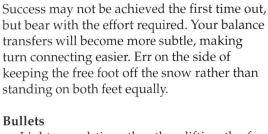

Fig. 5-7. Parallel garland on easy terrain

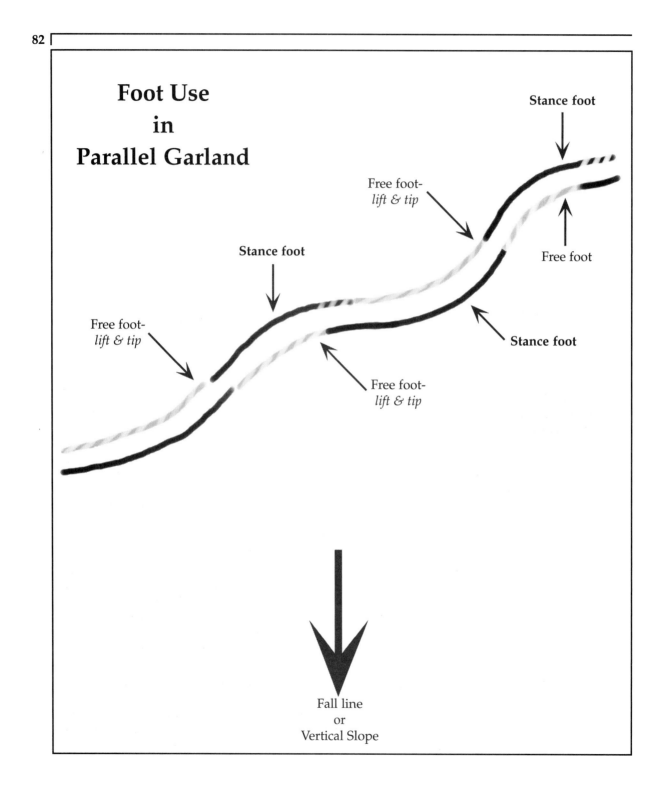

Foot Use
in
Parallel Garland

Stance foot

Free foot-
lift & tip

Free foot

Stance foot

Stance foot

Free foot-
lift & tip

Free foot-
lift & tip

Free foot-
lift & tip

Fall line
or
Vertical Slope

Chapter 6 - Release to Full Turn

The foundation has been laid, the components are in place; now we make the whole turn. Good ski turns include a release, transfer, and engagement. These actions are a simple matter of flattening, lifting, and tipping the ski. In this chapter you'll practice the complete turn with an edge change from a standing start.

You are now prepared to go through the transition and continue into a serious carved arc. Fortunately, turns made using primary movements require no technical mind exercises. If you want to turn to the right, make the phantom move with the right foot. Knowing how to use these movements eliminates the need to learn all kinds of other traditional teaching concepts like rotary, twisting, or skidding maneuvers.

I believe there is a place for skidding, but only if taught correctly. Skidding can be valuable when properly directed and controlled with primary movements. Skidding should utilize ski shape and design. You may actually have some skidding in your first efforts to complete phantom turns, but it will be controlled and progressive, based on the movements you have already learned. Refining the movements will increase performance by increasing ski to snow edging angles. The legs or upper body are kept in balance by generating the ski movements through actions close to the snow. Any sign of a skid will disappear and you will develop the control demonstrated by all great skiers.

Introducing the primary movements to experts has immediately been an enlightening experience for them. Friends and clients alike have amazed me with their varied understanding of skiing movement. Although considered experts, they often make movements that are inefficient and energy consuming. After they practice the primary movements for as little as half an hour they present a completely different picture of skiing. Observers have often commented that they can pick out skiers who are skiing with primary movements, spotting them from the top of the slope. They demonstrate an elegant, efficient skiing picture. Their turn arcs leave clean, round tracks in the snow.

"Primary movements skiers just look… different; they use the ski through the whole turn."

Craig McNeil, former pro bump skier, ski writer, instructor

If you are an advanced skier and have never gone through the beginning of this progression, take a review course of the early chapters so you can join in at this point and achieve instant results.

Previous:	*Parallel garland, free foot on snow*
6-1.	**Transition movements**
Next:	*Two footed release to full turn*

a   *b*   *c*

Fig. 6-1. Stationary tipping of feet from one set of edges to the other

In Brief

Here, we revisit the movements that started us on the path to efficient and elegant skiing. Basic tipping gains an additional feature: by lifting the stance foot, we transfer balance, making it a new free foot.

Details

Fig. a. Stand on a slight incline, using your poles for support. Balance on the stance foot and tip the skis to a high edge angle.

Fig. b. Begin to flatten both feet as in releasing.

Fig. c. As the skis become flat to the snow, pick up the stance foot to make it the free foot. Start to tip it toward the little toe edge.

Fig. d. Narrow your stance slightly to facilitate tipping.

Fig. e & f. The free foot is tipped onto the little toe edge preparing for the next turn.

Summary

Whenever you read "tip it toward the little toe edge", that action is with the free foot. In every case this means the other foot has become the stance foot. The free foot should always lead the action of tipping. This movement, done early and aggressively, can make the legs look bowed, showing a gap between the knees.

As we start to connect turns a transfer occurs early in every transition. Primary movements are the tools to make the transition easy, because you are entering the turn balanced on the new stance foot. The tipping exercise here demonstrates how the actual transition progresses. Practicing this movement rehearses sensations needed for turn transition. This transition sequence is in every turn and is a key to success; familiarize yourself with it to save weeks of lessons.

d   *e*   *f*

Bullets

- While stationary, perform releasing, transferring, and engaging movements

You learned to use the release to begin the turning process. Now, refine the movement and transfer balance early in order to engage carving earlier in the turn. Releasing is the action that begins parallel turns on shaped skis. The next step is to transfer and engage higher in the arc. The goal of this chapter is to connect releasing to engaging. The time between the two will be reduced as you experience the movements in this chapter. The shorter the transition time, the better your balance for the next turn.

Fig. 6-2. Two footed release to turn - complete

In Brief

Release and transfer balance to the new stance foot before the skis head directly down the slope. Release by lightening the free foot. Engage the new stance ski by tipping the free foot - using the phantom move.

Details

Fig. a. Begin with a two-footed, flattening release from a standing position across the slope.

Fig. b. Direct the ski tips down the slope.

Fig. c. Flatten the skis further and prepare to lighten and create a free foot with the lower ski (skier's left foot).

Fig. d. Feel the skis flatten to the snow.

Fig. e. Pick up the stance (skier's left) foot and make it the free foot; balance on the new stance foot.

Fig. f. Balancing on the stance foot allows increased tipping of the free foot.

Fig. g. Pull the free foot closer to the stance foot to help with the tipping action. Flex the knee of the free foot and tuck the free foot back under the body.

Fig. h. Begin to lower the tail of the free ski in order to spread fore/aft balance over the whole foot.

Fig. i. Keep the free foot light and continue to tip it toward the little toe edge. Start to feel more pressure toward the heel of the stance foot.

Fig. j & k. Finish the turn by continuing to tip the free foot toward the little toe edge. Keep the free foot light and gently brushing the snow as you approach the finish.

Summary

Stand solidly on the new stance foot before you aim straight down the slope. The all-important free foot directs the rest of the turn. The finish of the turn depends on how long you want to continue tipping the free foot. By taking this movement to the extreme on some models of shaped skis one can carve full 360's all the way back up into the slope and around. Typically, you'll end sooner and go right into another release in the opposite direction to connect turns.

Bullets

• Commit balance to the new stance ski before you head straight down the slope

• Complete the whole turn with the free foot off or skimming the snow

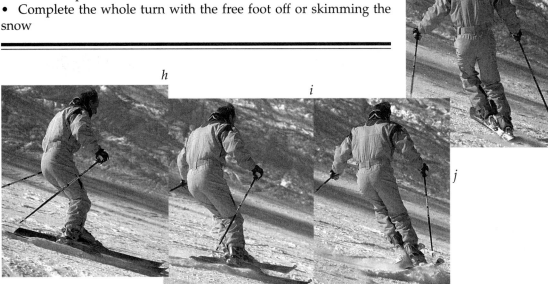

Previous: *Two footed release to full turn*
6-3A.   Two footed release to turn - beginning
Next: *Two footed release to turn - midsection*

In Brief

The next three photo series demonstrate three separate sections from one turn. The previous exercise described the movements being performed. Here, for the detail-oriented reader, the minutiae required to achieve the next level are painstakingly described. Minimize dependence on an extended, two-footed release. Start to lighten the free ski as soon as possible, working toward a refined release right into an engaged ski. The photos still demonstrate a two-footed release, but as you start moving, connecting turns, and adding speed, earlier transfers can be achieved. The goal is to get the ski engaged before the tips are headed straight down the slope. The earlier the ski is engaged, the sooner the ski goes to work, therefore the dynamics of the turn are heightened.

Details, 6-3A: Beginning of Turn

Fig. a. Flatten both skis to release, but start sooner with the stance foot (skier's left); this will draw the free foot into action. The free foot shouldn't be tipped too far. The stance foot should flatten progressively as the ski tips head down, but as on a snowboard, be aware that if the ski tips beyond flat before it turns, its little toe edge will catch on the downhill side.

Fig. b. Keep the activity of flattening gradual, sensing the flat, slippery skis under you as you move down towards the fall line. All the flattening is created by foot activity, tipping the stance foot toward the little toe.

Fig. c. Flatten farther using gravity to draw the skis toward the fall line at this point. As you feel the skis turning, flatten them as much as possible without rolling onto the big toe edge of the free foot. If you feel comfortable at this point in the turn, start to transfer. Move your balance toward the free foot (skier's right) by lightening the stance foot (skier's left). The skis will turn more quickly and easily now.

Fig. d. The skis should feel very slippery at this time in the direction change. This is crux of the transition. Here you must create the transition with a transfer of balance. The transition happens more easily and is more assured with increased speed.

Fig. e. The transfer or switch of balance to the new stance foot is complete. The free foot (skier's left) has already started to tip toward its little toe edge (indicated by the increase in distance between the knees).

Fig. f. The stance ski is completely engaged and committed to the new turn, while the free foot is directing the turn.

Bullets

- Transfer before the release is complete

Fig. 6-3A. Two footed release to turn - beginning portion

Previous: *Two footed release to turn - beginning*

6-3B.   Two footed release to turn - midsection

Next: *Two footed release to turn - ending*

Fig.6-3B. Two footed release to turn, middle portion

Details, 6-3B: Turn midsection

Fig. a. Stay balanced on the stance foot as you progress into the turn. Keep the stance leg long at this point by pushing against the snow. Be sensitive to the bottom of the foot; pressure at the heel should increase as you extend the leg. Feel the pressure along the inside big toe side of the stance foot. Try to feel the whole length of the ski edge on the snow. On the heel, the ski should be tracking and feel heavy. Feel the ski tail gripping and stable without sideways movement as in skidding. Resist any collapsing, quick flexing, or turning actions of the stance leg.

Fig. b. The engaging part of the turn continues as the ski heads down the slope. Your body will move to the inside of the turn due to tipping actions of your free foot toward the little toe edge. Keep the free boot close to the stance leg. As your center of balance moves inside the arc it causes the ski to increase carving. A free foot lifted off the snow is your measure of balance.

Fig. c & d. Snow sprays off the bottom of the ski, throwing it to the side of the slope, in the direction of the camera: this means the ski is carving. Concentration at the top of the turn is particularly critical with shaped skis. Most shaped skis are shorter and lighter than our old boards. If skidding action of any kind is started with a leg twist or foot steering action, displacing the shorter, lighter ski, which is less resistant to skidding out, then the turn is lost. The twisting or spinning energy carries farther into the turn, to the point where gravity tends to augment the skid of the skis coming across the slope. The main forces we sense in skiing are gravity and centrifugal force. Their efforts combine near the bottom of the turn to pull the skier downhill. If the skis are skidding when they get to this point, they'll continue skidding, and an extended skid makes it doubly difficult to

d *e* *f*

connect turns. If all the snow spray from the ski comes at the end of the turn, pushing the snow downhill, you are skidding. Many skiers get into the habit of twisting the skis at the beginning of a turn, because they were taught that way. A skidding ski often reminds me of a spatula smearing icing on a cake, forming wide, sweeping brush marks. Narrow, slicing grooves are formed through precise lower leg and foot tilting activities.

Fig. e & f. You'll feel gravity's pull on your body more strongly as you enter the last part of the arc. The free ski takes on a different role in balancing through the bottom of the turn by preparing for the forces that are generated. The tail of the stance ski needs more weight at the bottom of the turn to keep it carving through the fall line. If you stay too far forward on the ski, due to excessive knee drive, forward lean, or pressure on the ball of the foot, the ski tip will be pressured, releasing the tail. In *fig. e* the tail of the free foot is lowered. This change has a significant effect on the body's fore/aft equilibrium, settling more weight toward the heel of the ski.

Previous: *Two footed release to turn - midsection*

6-3C.   **Two footed release to turn - ending**

Next: *One foot balance*

Details, 6-3C: Ending of turn

Fig. a-c. The forces discussed earlier add fun to skiing. The best part of the turn is the last third. The sensations of body lean and extreme inclination toward the slope generated with shaped skis were formerly felt only by the world's top skiers. Shaped skis make this feeling available at much slower, safer speed. The tilt angle of the free foot continues to increase to maintain carving.

Fig. d-f. Completing turns is really a lost art. The greatest fun and sensation in skiing is the sling shot effect you get when your skis accelerate out of the fall line across the slope. Use the arc to generate speed to get your skis across the hill into the next turn. The round completion of this turn is an arc, not a smear. Much of the thrill of snowboarding comes from the board rushing you out of the arc at the bottom of the turn. The feeling resembles a high G turn on a roller coaster. Now, with these skis, the high G turn feel is available at a much less threatening speed.

Fig. e. The body maintains a very relaxed position over the stance foot. The stance leg bears the body's weight and resists the forces of the turn, but the muscles are not burning because the leg and body are lined up skeletally. The bones, rather than muscular energy, hold the body upright. Skeletal alignment is important to achieve because it conserves strength, allowing for more fun and extended skiing time. The combination of proper foot and boot alignment, shaped skis, and the use of primary movements can produce this experience for skiers.

Fig. f. The end of the turn comes when the free ski is put back on the snow and the stance foot begins to flatten, as at the beginning of this exercise.

Bullets
• Finish the turn by lowering the tail of the free ski

a

Fig. 6-3C. Two footed release to turn - ending portion

One-Footed Skiing: A Prerequisite for Success

Misunderstanding abounds about skiing on one foot. For over a decade, ski instruction has expected and accepted minimal results from students. Ski teaching took a big step backward when it adopted the position that skiers need to stand on two feet to learn how to ski. In my opinion, it banished skiers to mediocrity. The two-footed "technique" arose from low expectations - if skiers can't stand on one ski, don't challenge or help them, just forget them. Teach them a lower level of performance: skiing on two feet. As a result, a whole technique was developed around two-footed skiing. If that's all you learn, you are guaranteed never to advance beyond the intermediate level.

I experienced a situation this season that is typical, and demonstrates a point accurately. An instructor who had attended a training session came to me asking about the training she received. She said that during the session the trainer taught the trainees, all instructors, to ski in a wide, two-footed stance on shaped skis. The trainee instructor was confused about that approach, since only the previous day, I had successfully taught her to use a one-footed balanced stance, with which she had a major breakthrough in her skiing. She then commented that when the trainer skied in front of the group on a free ski run, he skied with his feet closer together, lifting his free ski off the snow. In short, he was teaching the dogma, but not allowing it to destroy his karma.

> *"Skiing on one foot: as I learned, it's the key to skiing in balance. At first, it felt wrong, but with what I learned from Harald, I realized that I had been out of balance since the first day I put on skis despite thousands of dollars worth of lessons. Now, I feel totally in control and can carve turns on black runs for the first time in my short skiing career."*
> *Jim Pitcock, MD*

Our experience with thousands of skiers in our Alignment Systems has conclusively demonstrated that better than ninety percent of the skiing population can benefit from an alignment program. Ten percent are very close to good alignment, but in many cases they can still benefit. When alignment is evaluated, one-footed balancing exercises are included. Skiers who get aligned and introduced to one footed balance improve quickly. Spending time and money to get aligned is rewarded by the reduction in frustration and learning time.

Every expert or elite skier I know skis balanced on one ski and can link turns on one ski. I always teach my students how to stand on, and ski on, one foot. If they are not able to do so, I align them. After the alignment they are able to ski on one ski. Consequently, their learning rate increases. If you have the ability to balance on one ski, yet you learned to ski with your feet in a wide, two-footed stance, I can sympathize with you and promise you better days ahead.

My life has been devoted to producing top ski racing athletes. I started coaching because I was a racer and I felt that if kids were going to train hard and dedicate themselves, they deserved coaching that would make them successful. My athletes were always the best skiers on the mountain and I am fortunate to have coached some of our country's best racers. Now that I have changed my focus to teaching the all-around skiing population, I feel that the skiing public deserves quality teaching and teaching systems that reward the students' efforts. The ability to stand on one foot will determine how quickly you move to the next level of skiing. Lito Tejada-Flores, whom I believe has made a bigger contribution to ski teaching than any other person or organization in the past two decades, operates special ski camps. We started to align Lito's clients last season. Now, Lito has incorporated the alignment system into the camp program. Lito believes that balancing on one ski is a key to improvement, and he makes sure his students are equipped to achieve this balance.

The next exercises will develop your ability to balance on one foot. Every skier should be capable of performing them. The ability to turn on one ski should be your highest skiing goal. It defines a high level of skiing proficiency. Don't give up, you may need some practice. Most people are better on one foot than the other. This usually indicates that there is an alignment improvement available on the more difficult side.

Fig. 6-4A. Traverse on one foot

In Brief

Practice a straight run on flat smooth snow, balancing on alternate feet (no photos). Do the same as shown in a traverse.

Details

6-4A, fig. a & b. Push off on one side of the slope, headed in a shallow traverse. Set the stance foot on edge. When you feel comfortable, pick up the uphill foot (skier's right) making it the free foot. Try this in both directions. Your ski should cut a single edge line in the snow on the traverse.

6-4A, fig. c & d, and *6-4B, fig. a-c.* Traverse with both feet on the snow and gradually lighten the stance or downhill foot (skier's left). At first, lift only one part of the stance foot (heel or toe) cleanly off the snow. If you are able to do this, continue to traverse while trying to lift the whole ski.

Summary

This exercise can be difficult. It may take practice until you can perform it. Don't give up. I have used it with intermediate skiers of all abilities and ages, and it works. If you are having difficulty with these exercises and are interested to know why, read the alignment section of the book, Chapter 12.

One-footed balancing is important because it makes the transition, a difficult part of the turn, easier. Expert skiers go through the transition of the turn very quickly. The less advanced skier's transition takes longer and can be problematic. For a moment, in every transition, even the expert skier has to rebalance and make a move to switch stance from one foot to the other; this is the transfer.

Fig. 6-4B. Traverse on uphill foot

Commitment to the movement that takes you from one balance foot to the other is the key to a successful transition. You have worked on building these movements and combining them. Comfort and security in the transition phase are based on one-footed balancing ability. The next exercise will demonstrate the timing and movements needed to make successful transfers.

Bullets
- Traverse on stance foot with free foot lifted
- Transfer by lifting the former stance foot, then traverse on the new stance foot
- If you can't traverse in a straight line without difficulty, read the alignment section

Here I demonstrate the combination of immediate lifting and tipping as an evolution of the simultaneous, two-footed releasing movements. These movements are closer to the early balancing and transferring movements that great skiers use. Elite skiers are difficult to emulate because they hide the subtle but all-important linking movements that make all the difference in getting to their level. This exercise points out these movements and builds them for your skiing.

Fig. 6-5. Full turn

In Brief

Push off at a steep angle headed away from the fall line. Lift and tip the stance foot (skier's right) keeping the ski tip on the snow. Use the phantom move to complete the turn.

Details

Fig. a & b. Start at a steep angle headed away from the fall line. Push off to get some speed before you make any moves. Stand on the stance foot (skier's right).

Fig. c. Pick up the stance foot and allow the new stance foot (skier's left) to go flat to the snow.

Fig. d. Lifting only the tail of the free foot, immediately tip it to the little toe side.

Fig. e. Let your balance achieved naturally on the new stance foot take you around the turn.

Fig. f. Continue to tip the free foot and at the same time pull it in closer to the stance boot.

Fig. g-i. Now you can start to lower the free foot, bringing it back to the snow. This will help to bring your balance gradually back to the mid-foot and heel to finish the turn.

Summary

The tendency is to rush the stance ski into a turn to get it across the slope. Be patient. Do not twist, turn, or otherwise disturb the stance leg. If you come from a background of ski lessons that emphasized rotary movements or leg twisting, you are in for a major change. You have the opportunity to improve your skiing substantially. When the tail follows the tip we call it carving. With old technology skis, twisting was the standard technique in ski instruction. Few instructors really teach carving because it is difficult to achieve. It was the domain of the racer. Now, everyone has the opportunity to carve. If you show up for a lesson with shaped skis and the instructor is talking about foot twisting and leg turning for any turn, run, don't walk, to another instructor or ski school.

Bullets

- Release from the new stance foot
- Use free foot tipping to engage the turn

6-6.   Two footed immediate release

Here I demonstrate how both feet release but one-footed balance begins turn entry. Because the exercise is for demonstration purposes, it is done slowly and deliberately to highlight the key movements used by elite skiers. Movements made by the best skiers are difficult to observe because these skiers often keep the free foot close to the ground, and move it subtly. If you have the opportunity to watch a World Cup race or a video of the best slalom skiers in the world, you will see the exact movements that are demonstrated here. In particular, the Austrian World Cup winners use and demonstrate these movements. The Austrian ski team has the most advanced and directed technical program of all the Alpine Nations. They consistently dominate the technical events on the World Cup. This is no coincidence: they teach and train their athletes efficient movements.

Why, you might ask, are we trying to learn movements used by the elite skier and racer? It has been the convention that the movements of elite skiers are beyond the capabilities of the recreational skier. I have demonstrated to clients and instructors that this need not be the case. Efficiency and functionality are the hallmark of elite skiers. The goal of the Primary Movements Teaching System is to teach the efficient and functional movements of expert skiing.

In Brief

Bring the skis flat from the edged position of the prior turn. Immediately lift the stance foot and tip it toward the little toe side. The new stance foot is created before the turn has begun.

Details

Fig. a. From a traverse, carry all balance on the stance foot (skier's left).

Fig. b. The free foot is on the snow. Tip both feet flat and pick up the stance foot; this action exchanges the roles of the feet. I now have a different stance foot. Use the pole plant for additional support.

Fig. c. Tip the free foot in advance of the stance foot. Get the free ski over to its little toe edge and touch the ski tip to the snow.

Fig. d. Pull the free foot aggressively toward the stance boot while keeping the tip of the free ski on the snow. The stance ski is comfortably engaged.

Fig. e. Slowly bring the free foot back in contact with the snow but don't put weight on it. Continue to tip it to the little toe side.

Summary

The belt buckle on my suit, starting in the first photo of the sequence, starts on the uphill side of my boots then moves across and over the skis to the inside of the turn. Who said, "move your center of mass?" How does one do that? None of this was achieved by attempting to move the body. It is the result of correct movements at the feet and the kinetic chain readjusting links higher in the body to maintain balance.

Fig. 6-6. Two footed release to turn, green terrain

In *fig. b* to *d*, notice the free foot tipping toward the little toe side before the stance foot matches it. This is indicated by the greater space between the knees then the boots. The movement of the free foot is an aggressive and necessary component of expert skiing. Here the action is so quick that the knee of the free foot ends up pointed down the slope (this results from tipping the foot, so don't try to move the knee). The ski tip is also touching the snow on its little toe side. A point to clarify is the action of the free foot or leg. In traditional teaching, rotary or twisting actions of the free foot leg (skier's left) are emphasized. You may hear phrases such as steer or turn the inside leg or foot. Rotation of the free foot leg is erroneous and has a negative impact on ski performance. Free leg steering rotates the body and disrupts balance. Free leg steering diverges the ski unless you rotate the stance leg to keep up, which causes the stance ski to skid.

If you are on track to learning how to carve and ski parallel with the correct movements, why start rotating any part of the body? Let the body take care of its own needs and use the design of the ski, through the use of primary movements.

The pole plant gives extra support and stability to the stance foot as it rolls to the new edge. The role of the ski pole is critical to the success of the parallel turn. Refer to Chapter 9 on pole use for a complete introduction.

Bullets
- Transfer to uphill, little toe edge of new stance foot
- Tip directly to engaged big toe edge of stance foot using phantom move

Movement progression continues on following page

Previous: *Two footed immediate release*

6-7. **Uphill foot release to phantom move**

Next: *Linked, medium radius turns*

Traversing on one foot, either on the uphill or downhill ski, is an important component of your skiing education. As presented in exercise 6-5, balancing the body over a one-footed stance can lead to major advancement in your skiing. This particular exercise can be a breakthrough event. Skiers use it regularly to test their balance and refine their skiing. It often introduces a new sensation in skiing. It is a new challenge and it will raise your skiing standards.

In Brief

Transfer balance to the new stance foot while in a traverse. Tip the free foot to start the turn.

Details

Fig. a. Start from a traverse on the uphill stance foot. Raise the free foot clearly off the snow and experiment with tilting the ski tip up and down.

Fig. b. Draw the raised leg in and lower that ski tip.

Fig. c. Tip the free foot actively toward its little toe edge. Balance on the stance foot allowing the actions of the free foot to angle the skis into the turn.

Fig. d. While solidly edged on the stance ski, keep the back of the free ski raised. Speed and momentum from the turn keep me balanced and ready to develop more inclination.

Fig. e. Engage the stance ski into a deep carve by extending the leg.

Fig. f. Keep the free foot in contact with the stance foot and tucked back under the body. Don't leave it to dangle out and away from the body. Now the stance ski has caught up to the tip angle of the free ski.

Fig. g. Fore/aft balance is controlled by the actions of the free foot learned through our exercises of raising and lowering its tail. Lower the tail of the free ski, centering the body. As the turn heads back into and across the slope, stand directly over the heel of the stance foot for a strong carved finish.

Summary

In the traverse before the turn the free ski tip started in a higher position than the tail, then the tip dropped before the free foot started the tipping action toward the new turn. Pushing the tip down centers the body at beginning of a turn.

Standing on the heel through the middle of the turn by extending the leg moves your balance to the back of the foot, but it does not mean to sit back. As described in earlier exercises in this chapter, after *fig. g,* lower the free foot to prepare it to become the new stance foot. Lift the **present** stance foot and start the whole process again for a new turn.

Bullets
- Traverse on little toe edge of uphill stance foot
- Engage by using phantom move from a moving traverse

Fig. 6-7. Uphill foot traverse to phantom move

Chapter 7 - Linked Turns

"I am eminently grateful to the instructors and the instruction methods of this program. It distills instruction to the essential elements, eliminating the complexities that confuse the student. As a result I have progressed from what I thought was terminal intermediate status to advanced level skiing."
      David Disick, President, Franz Klammer Lodge

We have reached linked, carved, turns. Medium and short-radius arcs are turns many skiers aspire to make. All the photos in this chapter were taken from the same continuous run. If you have had any ski instruction you will have seen this turn described, analyzed, demonstrated, and dissected. Are you bored yet? I am. Not here, though. I won't bore you with dull descriptions. The carved, medium-radius turn is important, so let's bring it to life. This chapter could be titled,

"Everything you ever wanted to know about the carved turn, but couldn't find anyone to tell you."

Soon, you'll learn how to perform this turn with the new shaped skis. You've never heard it described this way before, so hold on, because the shaped skis are changing skiing. These turns don't start with a rotation or twist, because we don't want to develop any "graceless scrapers" here.
      Everything you have read and learned from the previous chapters will be used here to elevate your skiing to a new performance level. If you skipped to this chapter to see how the elite skier makes turns, don't turn back now. Go ahead, try it; you may be in for a surprise. Once you've tried the movements you can decide to go back to previous chapters for a briefing.

Parallel skiing is no longer the elusive goal. I take it for granted that this system can produce parallel skiing very quickly, given the new skis and the complete system. I'm raising the bar, tossing down the glove. The new goal is to perform graceful, carved arcs that leave round grooves etched into the newly groomed snow. If you already aspire to this performance, then let's roll.

For years, ski instruction avoided the carved turn, tossing around comments like: "Carving isn't everything", "There is more to skiing than carving", and "Here's another guy with a carving fetish - he probably can't ski anything else." I've heard it all, mostly from the upper echelon. Comments like these arise to mask the fact that carving is difficult to teach. I teach carving to my students and they love it. I'm reminded of the ongoing argument and controversy over skiing on one ski or with the feet together. Let's not teach it because the students can't do it. Low expectations of student performance combined with an ineffective teaching system yield poor skier performance! This is similar to a fellow telling his wife she can't have a Porsche, claiming that "Porsches are too fast, and impractical", when he actually is unable to teach her how to use the clutch. What a loss to save face.

You have already been introduced to most of the movements needed to carve linked turns. You may already be carving if you have followed the lessons in this book. The movements that produce carving are the same as those for all around solid skiing. Carving movements give you the versatility to ski on all snow, on all terrain. Now, refine and combine movements to produce the skiing you desire, whether it be extreme carving, bumps, powder, crud, all-mountain or "off-piste". Don't get frustrated by what you may have been taught before, let's get on with the good stuff.

The direct, carved, parallel turn entry is easy to learn once the gradual release entry you practiced in the previous chapter is mastered. The gradual, two-footed release entry has a hesitation before the ski is engaged. That release does have a segment in the middle where the skis are flat to the snow, and the ski's edges don't engage until further down in the direction change. It's just the learning phase you go through to get to direct engaging. Linking carved turns requires an immediate transfer. The releasing movements you learned earlier lead to direct, quick releases using the phantom move. Hesitation at the top of the carved arc is gone.

All of the photos in this chapter were taken from the same series of turns. The turns are round because these are shaped skis and they carve round turns. In fact, these skis don't really like to go straight. They don't need any "twisting" help to start into a turn. They actually lose their effectiveness and carving ability if they are twisted. In fact, only tipping will create the turn arc you about to see and learn.

In Brief

Relax the stance leg to release into the turn. Use the phantom move of the free foot to engage and direct the turn.

Details

Fig. a. This is the finishing phase of the previous turn. Stand on the stance foot (skier's right). The free foot is maintaining close contact with the stance foot.

Fig. b. Look down the slope to pick out exactly where you want to place the next turn.

Fig. c. Place the free foot on the snow and start to **relax** the muscles of the stance leg.

Fig. d. Stand completely on the old free foot (skier's left) and pick up the new free foot (skier's right). The support previously provided by my stance foot to keep the body uphill of the skis is gone, therefore the body moves down the slope, pulled by gravity and momentum. This is a great feeling. It requires no effort, just relaxation.

Fig. e. Tip the new free foot.

Fig. 7-1. Linked, medium-radius turn on blue terrain

Fig. f. Contract the muscles of the new stance leg (skier's left) to develop support and strength in the new turn. Avoid bending or flexing that leg or the turn will weaken.

Fig. g. The beauty of this turn is gravity doing virtually all the work. Continue to perform the phantom move, tipping the free foot.

Fig. h. All of the body's balance is on the stance foot. Flex the free leg to shorten it and clear the way for body inclination as you round the corner.

Summary

Relax: Relaxing the muscles of the stance leg at the bottom of the turn starts the releasing of the stance ski.

After all these years of being told to relax, here's how, when, and why. The stance leg shortens or flexes as the relaxed muscles provide less resistance to gravity. Relaxing is an important strategy in connecting turns smoothly. The act of relaxing starts to transfer balance to the free foot, creating even pressure between the feet. Relaxing also causes the stance ski to flatten, starting the release.

Once the stance ski is flat, it won't continue toward the little toe on its own accord. Help it with the transition. Roll progressively from flat to a tipped ski on the little toe edge in one continuous movement. This tipping of the free foot after the release engages carving on the new stance foot. You enter the carving zone.

Stance width: In *fig. g*, although the feet are apart, this is not a wide stance. This image often leads to misunderstanding about a wide stance. The vertical distance between my feet has increased (the free foot is lifted) but the free foot is still touching the stance leg. It is important to increase the vertical distance between the feet to encourage body inclination, and to prevent the free foot from dragging on the snow. Stance width, or horizontal distance between the feet, should be determined by

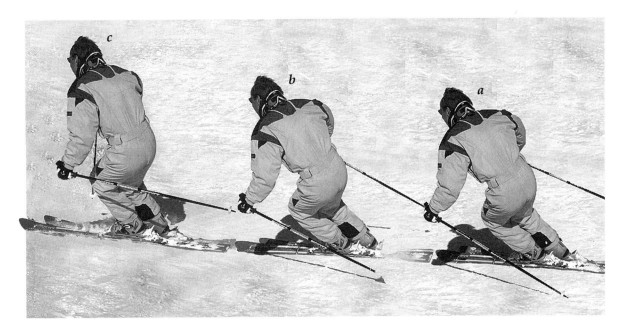

balancing needs. Increasing the width between the feet for contrived positional directives isn't necessary for an aligned skier, nor does it result in efficient primary movements. A wide stance reduces dynamic balancing ability and ski carving performance, especially at the top of the arc. A wide stance is completely nonfunctional in moguls, powder, or crud, and it looks awkward and graceless. Elegance is an attribute of skillful skiing and it is espoused by the Primary Movements Teaching System.

In this chapter, we discuss the necessary basic movement elements of transition and transfer. Engaging results from active continuation of lateral movements started at the snow level by the feet. During the release, gravity's pull provides assistance. Utilize the natural forces provided by the mountain environment to create efficient turns. This reduces energy expended, the need for leg strength, and disruptive power movements.

Bullets
- Relax to release
- Pick up to transfer
- Tip to engage

Previous: *Linked, medium-radius turns*

7-2.   **Transfer in linked, medium-radius turns**

Next: *Linked, medium-radius turns (continuation)*

Fig. 7-2. Transfer through turn in Fig. 7-1, frames b through e.

The photos here are shaded to demonstrate transfer of balance from one foot to the other. The darker shade is the stance side where the body is balanced. In reality, there isn't a sharp delineation between the stance and free sides of the body as is drawn in this sequence, but this does illustrate how the support is transferred. Since the transfer is such an important activity in our skiing, we use these round, medium radius, medium speed turns to show a gradual transition.

In Brief
Switch stance feet by relaxing the leg muscles of the stance leg and lightening the stance foot. Contract the muscles of the free leg, preparing it to support the body for the entry to the turn.

Details
Fig. a. Balance is on the stance foot; sense all pressure on that foot. Keep the free foot unweighted and skimming over the surface.

Fig. b. Relax the muscles of the stance leg (skier's right) to flatten that ski and transfer balance.

Fig. c. Lighten that ski to make it the free foot for a complete transfer. Equal shading means stance pressure is moving toward the new stance foot (skier's left).

Fig. d. Establish a new stance foot by picking up the free foot. The free foot can now perform its magic, starting the phantom move.

Summary
A standing start release as in Chapter 6 requires more patient, progressive flattening. Flattening in linked turns is almost immediate, with no time to hesitate. Momentum and gravity help to flatten the skis by pulling the body downhill as the skis tip under it. Lateral tipping movements started at the feet move up the kinetic chain and produce balance, transferring it from one leg to the other.

But how do the skis create the turn? The side cut of the skis in the photo series produces a 12 meter turn radius. When the edge bites into the snow and is pressured with the body's weight, the ski bends and cuts an arc - this is the turn. At all costs, avoid turning the stance leg to tip toward the big toe edge as a means of engaging the ski (most skiers learn this movement first); this leads to a perpetual skidded wedge entry.

Contract the hamstring muscles on the back of the stance leg to move the hips slightly forward as a re-centering move. The idea is not to push away from the snow with the contraction. Rather, flex the hamstring muscles to pull your boot back under the body and move the hips forward. This is not a gross movement: think "re-center", not "thrust forward". It happens during the lateral edge transition, when the hips move from uphill of the skis to downhill of them, and when pressure and sliding resistance are minimized, making it easier to hold the feet back to re-center. Simply hold your feet back under the body to maintain fore/aft balance during transition.

The movements in this book, when performed as described, produce a correct, parallel, carved turn. There is simply no possible alternate outcome or result. The movements are biomechanically accurate. If you pick up one foot, you will stand on the other. If you release the stance leg, lift it, and start a phantom movement, you will engage an edge on the new stance ski. If you engage the edge of a shaped ski and balance on it, the ski will turn. These are simple concepts. They work, they're easy to understand, and they're easy to learn and use. We teach them successfully to all skiers. A correct skiing foundation is built on these movements and will head you to immediate and future progress. You won't have to unlearn movements ever again.

Bullets
- Refine and combine exercise 7-1
- Stay centered by contracting the hamstring to hold the feet under the body in the turn transition

7-3.   Linked, medium-radius turns (continuation)

The photos on the next two pages demonstrate the huge leap in performance that the shaped ski engineers have bestowed on us. Skiers have much to be happy about in skiing. If it weren't for these new skis, snowboarding would have taken over of the slopes. I would be snowboarding. I can't remember arcing turns like this on the old technology equipment without tremendous effort and speed. Further discussion of shaped skis is offered in Chapter 12.

Momentum and Gravity: Trust them

In Brief

Connect round turns by using primary movements to release, transfer, and engage.

Details

Fig. h-k. The stance ski is slicing into the snow, cutting the arc of the turn. Balance is on the stance ski. The thought is to stand centered on the stance foot and tighten the arc. Tighten the arc by applying extra pressure to the ski. How? Tip the skis to a greater angle and extend the stance leg. Keep tipping the free foot to the little toe side as you shorten the free leg by flexing it further under the body.

Fig. l-p. In *fig. l,* start relaxing the stance leg (skier's left) and feel its support diminishing. Pressure from the turn is diminished; feel the base of support disappearing and the leg becoming free. Now it becomes the new free ski; lift the back of that ski slightly and tip the foot aggressively toward the

Fig. 7-3. Continuation of linked turns from Fig. 7-1

little toe. The tip of the free ski, in contact with the snow, rolls from the big toe edge to the little toe edge. Feel the tipping and engaging on the new stance foot. This new stance ski (skier's right) rolls from the little toe edge of the ski, to flat, and immediately to the big toe edge in a distance of less than six feet between *figures m* and *n*.

Fig. 7-4. Continuation of linked turns from Fig. 7-3.

In Brief

Although the activities in this sequence are already described in detail in the earlier montages of this chapter, discussion here presents further insight.

Details

Fig. u-y. An active transfer and commitment is started by movements of the stance leg and foot. The angle of the body changes dramatically through these movements. Much discussion in ski teaching is focused on this part of the turn and how it is performed.

Summary

We must credit ski design for enabling such dramatic movement. On traditional technology skis, much higher speed was required to generate early ski engagement. The body position is a result of the ski performance. Racers and elite skiers could match this performance on traditional equipment with high levels of training, speed, and strength. Now, this level of dynamic skiing is available to the advanced skier at much slower speeds. Because the ski engages so early and cuts so sharply, you can commit to the ski. Because the ski starts arcing so quickly and tightly, in *fig. w*, it feels like a rope or force pulls you up the slope, holding you from falling. I teach my students to trust this pull. This type of skiing is great fun and doesn't demand great athletic ability. Use the movements and actions as described in this chapter to achieve these results.

Bullets

- Shorten the free leg as you tip the foot further into the turn
- Extend the stance leg to stay balanced

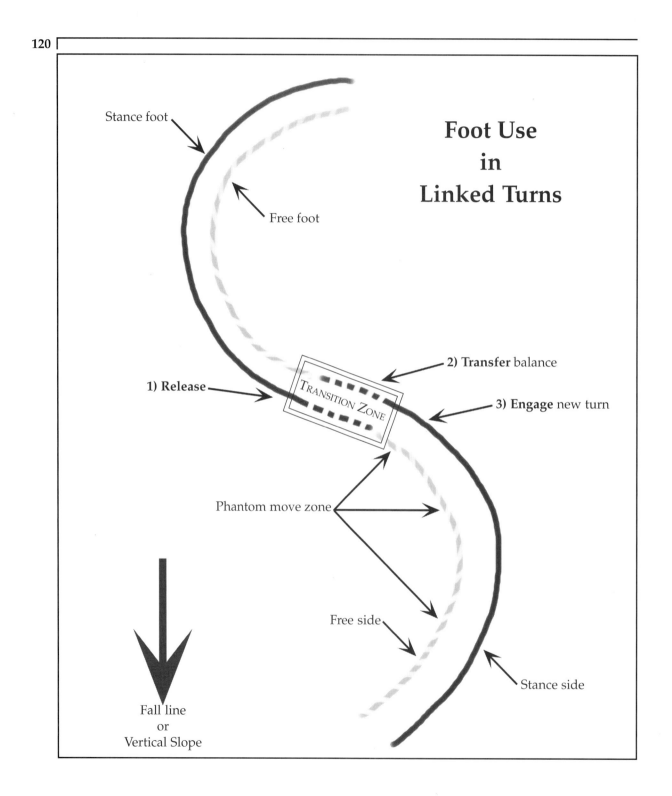

Stance foot

Free foot

**Foot Use
in
Linked Turns**

2) **Transfer** balance

1) **Release**

3) **Engage** new turn

TRANSITION ZONE

Phantom move zone

Free side

Stance side

Fall line
or
Vertical Slope

Chapter 8 - Linked Short Turns

Short turns, in my opinion, are the most fun and versatile turns for skiing. They display energy and excitement, and they require timing, quickness, and coordination. All right, let's not all start running for the exits; there's a place here for everyone, intermediate skiers included, and plenty of reasons for you to read this section. Great short turns are an attainable and realistic goal for all skiers now that the playing field has been leveled with equipment innovations and the Primary Movements Teaching System. Practicing the primary movements and developing the phantom turn has brought you to the threshold of success. The short turn is almost the same as the medium turn except the movements are continuous and come closer together in time and distance.

The basic short turn performed with primary movements creates the opportunity to ski terrain never before considered by the advanced skier. Experts - make short turns with a phantom move and breathe new life into your applications for this turn. Using my formula for short turns, you will energize your all-around skiing, just as the medium turn approach revolutionizes the carved turn. The short turn is the foundation for various off-piste situations including bumps, narrow steeps, powder, slalom, and ice. In Chapter 10, the direct application of short turns to bumps and powder is tested.

The new skis do present some interesting challenges for the skier with old movement patterns. By old, I mean those used by traditional teaching systems. Similarly, primary movements aren't really new, they simply haven't been considered the formal way to teach the skiing public. Now that the shaped skis are here, correct technique is essential if all the features built into the skis are to be used. Lateral movements are the basis for shaped ski utilization. New, old, traditional, revolutionary; regardless of the name or origin, the object here is to inform skiers about valid methods of skiing that are particularly effective on shaped skis. No one wants to waste time or money on inefficient methods of skiing on shaped skis. These are truly brilliant products that enable you to ski in a manner previously reserved for the world class skiers. The technique taught in most ski schools today robs us of the shaped ski's brilliant performance. That is why this book was written and why I also call it

"The definitive shaped ski owner's manual."

Linked, short radius turns

Previous: *Linked, medium-radius turns*
8-1.   Cruising, short-radius turns
Next: *Aggressive, short-radius turns*

Fig. 8-1. Transfer in short radius turns

Fig. 8-1 demonstrates mellow short turns on blue terrain - the classic, graceful, energy-conserving short turn. These are cruising turns compared to the later ones where you really crank out a sharp, decreasing radius. The beauty of this turn is that with shaped skis it requires very little effort to link twenty to thirty at a time or until the slope runs out. The movements used here will produce the correct skeletal stacking to utilize the natural turning radius of the skis. Use minimal movement, and derive most of the impetus for the turns from gravity and momentum. There is no need to be concerned with assuming or achieving a certain body position. Initiate your movements at the feet, and let the kinetic chain determine what the rest of your body does.

In Brief

Relax to release by lifting the stance foot. Tip the new free stance foot to engage the turn.

Details

Fig. a. The bottom of the turn is demonstrated here. Prepare for the next turn in this part of the arc. In *fig. a*, the stance foot (skier's left) is still generating pressure and ski engagement to complete the turn.

Fig. b. Get ready to head in the other direction. Gravity will help bring your body from uphill to downhill of your skis if you relax the leg muscles. Use relaxation to start the transition by surrendering to gravity's pull. Imagine that a rope is attached at the middle of my body, where my belt buckle is located. The rope pulls in the direction of the arrow on the page. Flattening the stance ski's edge angle by letting gravity pull toward the arrow will get the job done.

Fig. c. Pick up the stance foot on the way to the next turn.

Fig. d. Tip the free ski and place it on its little toe edge.

Summary

Although the free foot in *fig. b* is on the snow, it is only lightly weighted. It becomes the new stance foot in the transition between *fig. b* and *c*. This happens quickly, over a short distance. You can practice and reinforce these transfer movements through foot quickness exercises. For example, make linked phantom moves on a gentle slope without much direction change. The Primary Movements Teaching System focuses on creating all the significant skiing actions with small muscles and movements, which makes it easy to perform the movements quickly. Upper leg and upper body parts are difficult to move quickly; once in motion, a large body part is difficult to control, adjust, or stop.

Imagine the stance leg in *fig. b* disappearing. In fact, when you relax the muscles in that leg and lift it off the snow, it can no longer act as the stance and support leg. Once the stance foot is eliminated, the free foot has to become the stance foot. The free foot, still on its little toe edge, takes over the job of balancing the body, and thus becomes the stance foot. Gravity pulls the body into the new turn as the support leg is eliminated, causing the free foot to change edge from the little toe to the big toe side as it becomes the stance foot. Using the phantom move with the new free foot and gravity's pull, roll onto the new edge to transfer into the next turn.

Stay centered

Staying centered on the skis requires only minor management. Imagine again that a rope is pulling me down the gravity line. What happens if I use my hamstring muscles to pull my feet back under my body? The rope pulls my body toward gravity, moving my hips over my feet. Holding the feet from moving forward at the transition of the turn keeps you centered on the skis.

Bullets

- Release to transfer to the little toe edge of the new stance foot
- Tilt the new stance foot to its big toe edge by using the phantom move with the new free foot
- Hold your feet under your body during transfer

Previous: *Cruising, short-radius turns*

8-2.   Aggressive, short-radius turns

Next: *Pole use*

Fig. 8-2A. Linked short radius turns on blue terrain

The photos in this series demonstrate an energetic turn connection. This is a decreasing radius short turn on a steep section coming to gradual flat section. Aggressive turns are important for versatility in many situations, especially in bumps or steeps. Two factors determine ability to perform a decreasing radius short turn: proper movements and an appropriate combination of equipment. Proper movements include the ability to increase pressure on the ski and make quick lateral changes. High performance skiing results from the combination of shaped skis and lateral boots.

Equipment is instrumental in achieving successful, carved, energetic, short and medium turns. Ski and boot features must be considered and tailored to your skiing needs. The ski's shape and flex characteristics, both longitudinal and torsional, determine how far you can bend it into a turn. A boot must transfer lateral movements and energy directly to the ski. Infinite varieties of skis and boots exist; the correct model for you must match your skiing movements. Knowing how to choose a boot that suits your needs can be complicated. Similarly, the performance characteristics of seemingly alike boots can differ markedly. The alignment and equipment section of the book, Chapter 12, contains information to guide your equipment decisions.

In Brief

Lift and tip aggressively for energetic short turns.

Details

Fig. a. The turn is completed with the ski bent.

Fig. b. Relax the leg muscles to release the ski. Contract the hamstring muscle, at the back of the leg, and the hip flexor, at the front of the hip, to shorten the stance leg (skier's left), as you pick it up to make it the free foot.

Fig. c. A strong phantom move is the ticket here.

Fig. d. Tip the free foot on edge before the stance foot. Don't be concerned about the stance foot yet. Start by tipping the free foot, allowing the stance foot to lag slightly. It will come to the edge a fraction later, but when it does, it will tip quickly, immediately creating a high edge angle. The stance leg (skier's right) should be extending to maintain snow contact while the upper body moves into the center of the next arc. This creates a long, well-positioned stance leg. All the necessary elements for a short energetic turn are in place. When the stance ski tips and grips, contract the muscles of the stance leg to make it a solid beam allowing no flexing. Pressure is transferred immediately to the ski, which reacts by bending. The bend takes you into a sharp arc.

Fig. e-g. Notice how the middle of my body is to the inside of the turn, yet the upper body is vertical or level and forms a reversed "C" on the stance side (as the arrow indicates). The methods that enhance this upper body use are presented in Chapter 9, "Pole Use". Be aware of the little toe edge of the free ski cutting the snow as the big toe edge of the stance ski provides support and balance.

Fig. h. Keep both skis tipped to the same angle in transition to the new turn; make the first move with the new free foot (skier's right). It tips right toward the little toe, to turn right. In this frame, a rebound off a small bump requires the edge change to be performed while the skis are off the snow.

Fig. i. As the stance ski lands, its edge is ready to support and start the next carved turn.

Summary

Fore/Aft Balance

In *fig. a*, my legs are more flexed and my stance is slightly more forward than in the previous exercise. Don't confuse forward stance with pressing the shin into the front of the boot. This, by the way, ranks right up there with skiing's most misunderstood concepts. I never push my shin into the front of my boot because that movement diminishes balance and ski performance. I simply bring my feet further under my hips at certain points in the arc to get more tip engagement. Flexing the hamstring muscle and pulling the feet back under the body brings my hips forward relative to my feet. This action engages the wide, shaped tip in the snow and bends the ski radically on the slope.

The shaped skis are shorter; if you "camp out" up on the tips, the tails will release. Pressuring the front of a shaped ski isn't nearly as critical as it was on the older technology skis. The shorter length of these skis makes them react very quickly to a forward weight bias, therefore it takes very little pressure on the ball of the foot to shorten the turn radius. This becomes especially obvious on steeper slopes. The best advice is to apply small amounts of pressure to the ball of the foot but to remain balanced close to the middle of the foot and ski. I use the fore/aft controlling mechanisms we've discussed earlier: lift the back of the free ski and tuck the free foot back and under the hips as it tips. These actions will meet ninety-nine percent of your forward pressure needs.

No, up isn't necessary!

There isn't sufficient time in short turns to let a rising body creep into the turn transition. Contracting the hamstrings and hip flexors at the releasing point will keep the legs bending, moving the hips across, rather than up.

Entering a new turn in balance requires inactivity of the stance foot and leg. Most teaching systems focus all turning efforts on that leg. The Primary Movements Teaching System uses a completely different approach! The job of the stance foot and leg in carved turns is to support.

In the introduction for this section the act of releasing to eliminate stance support is discussed. The free foot takes over the support role. The body stands on and is supported entirely by the free foot while it is still on its little toe edge. This achieves the transfer. Using primary movements diligently will train your body to create this early transfer. You can expect to perform correct movements in the correct order when signals are given to utilize the kinetic chain.

The action following the free foot becoming the stance leg is an extension. This activity lengthens the leg as the hips cross into the turn. The stance leg needs to be active in lengthening to maintain contact with the snow, but it is not active in pushing or extending to apply pressure to the ski or to the ground at this phase. Keep the ski light on the snow slicing into the surface. The body is resisting only minor forces at this point in the turn, so there is no reason to muscle the skis or be overactive with the stance leg. Let the free foot's fine tuning activities do the work.

Fig. 8-2B. Continuation of linked turns in Fig. 8-2A.

The portion of the turn where the stance leg is most active, apart from relaxing to release, is midway through the arc. Through this portion of the turn the forces start building. The stance leg should remain a constant length to resist the forces. If muscle contraction isn't strong enough, the leg will give in to the forces and shorten. If you think of making the leg longer just before the forces build, you get a head start on the forces. It is easy to give in if you aren't prepared to resist at the bottom of the turn when forces get heavy and powerful. Giving in by flexing absorbs energy stored in the ski and results in a flat turn finish. Sustain energy by carving a bent ski, not by flexing or shortening the leg.

At the bottom of the turn, just before the release, the muscles of the leg immediately change roles, from pushing against the snow resisting flexing, to relaxing for the release. Relaxing can be slow and progressive for longer turns or quick and aggressive for short energetic turns. In very short, energetic turns, releasing is so quick that the stance leg and foot must get out of the way by using a phantom move.

For years, skiers have been taught to turn their legs to begin a turn. Turning the legs requires them to be flexed. Flexing early or at the beginning of the turn diminishes support by the stance leg and eliminates pressure needed to bend the ski. The resulting turn is a skid, not a carved turn. The ski isn't engaged until it is too late, at the bottom of the turn, when it is aimed across the fall line. No wonder it is so difficult to ski bumps. Futile and frustrating stance leg steering is taught to people on shaped skis. Primary movements yield short turn performance for shaped skis. The Primary Movements Teaching System clearly represents an alternative to skiers who want better performance out of their skis and their skiing. Armed with these movements and effective short turns, we are almost ready to take on the bumps. Only one feature is lacking - proper pole plants, to be covered in the next chapter.

Bullets
- Quickly change roles of the stance leg by relaxing it
- Contract the muscles of the new stance leg
- Tip the free foot, flex to shorten the free leg
- Extend to maintain snow contact with the stance leg

Chapter 9 - Pole Use

The importance of hand, arm, and pole use is emphasized throughout the book. Actual pole planting movements are described in this chapter. Most skiers wait too long to learn proper pole use, hence we see rampant "pole abuse". You don't need to look very far. One lift ride at most ski resorts will reveal plenty of examples: arms swinging like a boxer, hands dragging by the sides, or baskets grinding into the snow, sending up rooster tails. When you take lessons or learn how to ski, little time is spent on developing proper arm position or pole planting skills. Initially, instruction focuses on getting people moving down the mountain; once people are skiing, they rarely come back for basic pole instruction. After skiing for awhile, new goals pop up, or your motivation for skiing changes. You might be driven to ski parallel or might want to get to the black diamond runs. In this rush to improve there can be development glitches. One of the most common is the "Pole Plant".

Proper pole plants help to link turns, while improper pole use can actually hinder development of parallel connected turns. Considerable progress can be made without a pole plant as long as the hands and arms are positioned properly. Skiing with the new, radical side cut skis has reduced the need for poles on groomed slopes. Some shaped ski pioneers don't use poles. I must admit, there is a certain amount of freedom gained without poles on the carving skis, especially those shorter than 170 cm. New options in skiing have developed recently due to the carving phenomenon. The super-short, specialty carving ski is just one example. However, in almost every other form of skiing including powder, crud, bumps, steeps, and ice, poles are indispensable. For this reason, we have included a comprehensive guide to pole use.

Pole discipline

I have tried to stay away from two words in this book: discipline and work. I didn't want to make readers feel like skiing is a drudge. Now that you are hooked, though, and have persisted to this point, I can bring up the "unspoken". The ski industry tries to portray everything to do with skiing as fun, never relating it to work, which you should leave at home, especially if you are on a ski vacation. The common rhetoric is "Come skiing at our area, everything will be fun, and you'll automatically ski by some kind of magic." Although skiing just for the sake of the experience is fun, it can be frustrating if more pleasure through performance isn't achieved. It is my experience that learning how to do anything well involves some concentration, attention, and dedication. Some effort or work is required to achieve success. If you started with the hand and arm positions as described at the beginning of the book, and have been diligent in maintaining those positions, you are well on your way. Otherwise, the positions introduced here will require some concentration - mental effort or "work".

Big benefits are in store if you have a strong pole plant. Pole plants enhance your balance and expand your ability to ski confidently in difficult snow conditions and terrain. A sense of connecting body movements to continuous downhill motion is achieved when pole use is integrated with the releasing actions that start new turns.

Previous: *Aggressive, short-radius turns*

9-1.   **Free side pole use**

Next: *Stance side pole use*

In this first exercise a strong hand position is developed. From the basic hand position, or home base, all other hand and pole activities can be performed with efficiency. If you already use a pole plant, *fig. a* is your starting point. If you are not currently planting your poles, start with *fig. b*. The hand and pole positions and movements in this exercise apply to every form of skiing. If you decide to run slalom, ski bumps, or ski powder, this foundation will prevail. The focus in Photo 9-1 is the uphill or free hand (skier's right). The free hand is on the free foot side of the body. Hand discipline helps establish upper body position relative to ski and leg angulation. The exercise also increases upper body awareness, and creates upper body angles needed to complement carving at higher speeds and on slick snow. Through better hand position and pole use, immediate increases in ski performance are felt. Holding the hands wide apart, or away from the body, is one of the key elements of controlling body position and enhancing balance. Look at any photo of an elite skier; whether it be World Cup, Extreme, or all mountain, the poles are held away from the body. Most untrained recreational skiers have their poles tucked against their sides, like chicken wings.

Fig. 9-1. Uphill pole activity after pole plant

Details

Fig. a. The pole plant is in the snow. The transfer is complete and the stance foot (skier's left) for the next turn is established. Keep the inside hand at the same height as the pole handle when the pole is vertical. Keep the pole tip in the snow as long as possible after it is planted. Move the inside hand forward and over the point in the snow where the basket touches, to ensure that the hand stays ahead of the hips entering the turn. This is a key movement, as most skiers let the hand drop to their side at this point.

Fig. b. If you are not presently using a pole plant, concentrate on the hand position from this frame forward. Keep both hands forward, above the belt, and held wide away from the body.

Fig. c. Turn the hand to bring the knuckles to face up. When you face the knuckles up, the pole shaft aims out to the side and the arm and pole shaft will be forward of the boots, preventing your arms from dragging.

Fig. d. Continue to aim your knuckles up as you progress into the turn. Start to move the free hand forward. Notice how the pole tip goes up the hill and keeps up with the ski boots throughout the turn. The idea is to keep the pole tip or basket even with the boots.

Fig. e & f. The hand is pushed forward to maintain its lead in the turn. The knuckles continue to face up as the knob at the top of the pole handle points toward the opposite hand. This action continues to move the pole tip and basket forward.

Fig. g & h. The turns for this practice exercise should be medium-radius, complete, and round, as demonstrated in this montage.

Summary

Although you are focusing on the hand and arm movements to obtain a position, it is not a rigid, fixed, stiff position. Notice the relaxed appearance of the demonstration even though the movements are emphasized for clarity. The hands and arms do move to keep up with the developing turn. The foot movements are most important, so make sure the free foot is creating all of the tipping and turning activity. Beware, it's easy to focus on the hands to the exclusion of the feet! The uphill pole can be dragged slightly across the snow to give feedback as to its position.

Bullets
- Use the wrist to move the pole tip
- Move hand forward over the point of pole plant
- Turn knuckles up to extend pole tip up the slope
- Move hand forward through turn

Previous: *Free pole use*

9-2.   Stance pole use

Next: *Pole & arm location for correct pole use*

Proper use of the downhill, stance side pole is equally important, but it's not effective if the uphill pole position isn't established. Proper use of the downhill hand sets the pace for timing of and entry to the next turn. Once proper hand discipline is achieved it is a simple matter to add the pole planting movements. Again, the hands are wide to enhance balance sensations and stabilize the upper body.

In Brief

To determine an effective hand position, imagine that the knob at the top of the pole handle is the single scoop on top of an ice cream cone. Keep the stance side hand in a position so the ice cream won't fall out of the cone. The correct position of the pole is maintained when the pole handle is held so as to prevent the ice cream from toppling off.

Details

Fig. a. Hold your hands high, above the belt line. Start tipping the skis with the free foot.

Fig. b. The stance side hand (skier's left) stays in the upright, ice cream cone position. The wrist of the stance side hand is flexed up toward the body as the turn progresses.

Fig. c. Without moving the rest of the arm, flex the wrist to move the tip of the pole forward (bring the back of your thumb toward your biceps muscle). Make the tip of the pole skim carefully on the snow.

Fig. d & e. Keep the arm and shoulder still. Active wrist movement and a slight elbow bend are needed.

Fig. f. Begin the pole plant movement; it initiates timing for transition to the new turn. The elbow and wrist are flexed back toward the shoulder, swinging the tip of the pole forward in preparation for the pole plant. There is no movement of the shoulder or body.

Fig. g. The downhill arm is now extended to plant the pole and the wrist opens and moves down the slope.

Fig. 9-2A. Outside pole use leading up to pole plant

(Details continued on next page)

Details (cont'd)

Fig. h. Once the pole reaches the snow, leave it "planted" so it can act as a balance point.

Fig. i. Move the hand down the hill. This hand is your guide into the next turn.

Fig. j. Move the hand and arm well ahead of the body. Keep the tip of the pole touching the snow for balance and use it as a reference point for gauging body inclination toward the hill.

Fig. k. The free side hand and arm continue to move forward, keeping the lead in the turn.

Fig. l. The stance hand (skier's right) now starts to move the pole tip slowly forward to catch up with the boots in preparation for the pole plant of the next turn.

Summary

For all pole plants you should focus on moving only the pole tip to prepare for and make the pole plant. All of the body movements focus on the wrist and occasionally the elbow. If you start with the hands in a good, home base position, only small movements are required to have successful pole action.

In as few as two ski runs I have seen substantial improvements in skiers practicing this movement. Those who use primary movements notice dramatic differences immediately. While it's in the snow, feel the support of the pole with your arm. This arm and pole can and should support your weight. In the bumps section of Chapter 10 you will realize how important this technique is. Move the hand over the pole while you ski past the point where it was planted. The hand must keep up with your forward momentum. The tip of the pole in the snow is the only part of you that has stopped. Move your hand forward at this point or it will get passed and caught behind the body.

Bullets

- Flex wrist up toward shoulder to move tip into position
- Swing pole tip with the wrist

Fig. 9-2B. Continuation of previous frame

Previous: *Stance pole use*
9-3.   Pole & arm location for correct pole use
Next: *Advanced skiing*

                                                 a   *b*

Fig. 9-3. Pole position through turn   *c*

Use wrist flex to move the pole tip through the turn. Without this technique, excess arm swing is rushed into action at the completion of the turn. Many skiers never develop a strong pole plant because they bring the arm and shoulder around to plant the pole.

A tennis analogy is perfect here. The player who never appears rushed on the court is the one who develops the racket position and swing while running for the ball. The player who runs with the racket dragging and dangling must then swing at the ball furiously, and looks rushed or out of rhythm. The same is true for skiing. Prepare for the pole plant throughout the turn.

Wrong (Fig. a-c)

Fig. a. Many skiers have problems with pole plant timing for the reason demonstrated in *fig. a*. The pole arm and pole tip are delayed in preparing for the turn.

Fig. b. A last second scramble to plant the pole results in a quick hand and arm drive in the direction of the turn. The arm drive disrupts balance and advances the shoulder, preventing movement toward the next turn. The body is blocked and must swing out and around the pole plant to get started toward the next turn.

Fig. c. Find the triangle laid out in the snow as a reference. The pole tip for the pole plant should stay behind the line that abuts the ski boot. In this photo the pole tip is too far ahead, pointing to the line adjacent to the ski tip. The shoulder, arm, and pole are blocking movement to the new turn.

d

e

Summary

Compare the positions described above to the ones on this page. The correct pole use demonstrates the tip reaching the snow with the shoulders open, enabling the body to move toward the next turn.

Correct (Fig. d-e)

Fig. d. The correct point of contact for the pole tip is demonstrated here, downhill from the ski boots. The wrist and elbow are flexed toward the shoulder and you can sight down the length of the pole to the point of planting.

Fig. e. With respect to the triangle, the tip of the pole is in the snow lined up with the boot.

Bullets

• Prepare for pole plant throughout the turn

Chapter 10 - Advanced Skiing

Bump Skiing

> *"After a pro freestyle career and thirty-five years of skiing I thought there wasn't much more I could do to improve my bump skiing. Was I wrong! I met Harald, he showed me Primary Movements and changed my equipment. Now that I use his methods I ski with more energy and less effort than at any time in my career."*
> *Craig McNeil, former pro bump skier, ski writer, instructor*

Every ski resort has bumps. Some resorts are famous for bumps, especially in Colorado where the mountains are big and the bumps are soft. I stayed away from bumps for the first few years in Colorado, figuring that I wasn't getting any younger. I wanted to save my remaining decades for high quality skiing that dished out less overall body abuse. Well, in the last two years I've changed my mind. No, I haven't found the fountain of youth, but I do go out looking for bumps.

Shaped skis have caused my change of heart. The new skis don't require the hard, quick, leg twisting movements needed on the longer, straighter, old technology skis. The radical side cut makes them turn when they are tipped to an edge. They are shorter, so not as much board needs to fit around the corner. I ski on either a 183 cm radical parabolic or 193 cm moderate side cut ski. Some skiers have told me they have difficulty finding the sweet spot on the new skis in the bumps. This is not the case for me: I think they take after the bumps like a Golden Retriever to a mud wamp. If you are over-twisting rather than engaging the edge, the shorter skis will windshield wiper their tails. Fortunately, the movements that you have learned throughout the book will let you appreciate the shaped skis in the bumps. We will concentrate on applying these movements in slow motion on small bumps before we attempt a full-blown attack on "The Wall."

Of course, a solid command of the primary movements will increase enjoyment in bumps. The least skied part of bumps is right after the lip because most skiers are in the air or skidding. You can transfer early and engage the ski for more control.

Check your leg twisting and steering at the door if you want bumps to be your ticket.

How is the transfer made? Easy, lighten the stance foot! This movement is absolutely wondrous for returning from a bump run with a smile. At first, speed must be well controlled. Keep the speed down by choosing gentle slopes. Once the transfer is made, patience is an undeniable necessity. Let the skis make the turn. When faced with imminent acceleration in a mogul field, most skiers become control freaks. Unfortunately, the more you try to control by conventional means, the less control you get. While at the top of a bump with the stance foot lifted you are in control. Use the phantom move to start any direction changes. The beauty here is that you are already balanced on the foot on which you will enter the turn. This step by step method works, but you have to trust it. If you get flustered and revert to the push, twist, and skid method, you're in for an unceremonious dumping.

I have worked with countless skiers on their bump technique, and their first comment is always, "Why doesn't everyone teach this technique?" My response is, "Wait. Soon everyone will!" Don't expect to ski the bumps like the photos on the next pages without some preliminary work on your movements before you go near them. If you have followed the book and can make an edge change by lifting and tipping the free foot, you are ready. If you are an advanced skier coming for a bump session, I'll teach you the primary movements first.

Most people give up on bumps because after a few turns they go too fast, tumble, and end up in a heap. I remember countless times while training ski instructors where they tried to ski bumps at a higher level than their comfort zone to prepare for certification requirements. They were using movement sequences that are taught to the public on flat terrain, without success. Experts don't use the movements that are typically taught in a bump lesson.

10-1.   **Phantom move off a gentle bump**

Turns in bumps should be easier than on flat slopes because of the lack of tip and tail contact at the top of the bump. If you crank and twist on the skis at the top of the bump they pivot so easily that the tails will run into the side of the next bump. Is there a more sophisticated way? Use a gradual entry, ease into the trough, let the skis scrape the side of the bump to gain valuable speed control. Don't worry about turning the skis, that's the easy part; let's work on control. Remember the phantom move because it works in the bumps! Even if you've never made a parallel turn on groomed slopes, you can experience it for first time on a gentle bump.

The pole plant is a key to success in the bumps. That's why it was introduced in the previous chapter. The hands are always held forward of the body. All of the movements are at the wrist and elbow. The pole and hand positions stabilize your upper body, letting you use the lower body for turning.

a   *b*

Fig. 10-1. Phantom move off a gentle mogul

In Brief
Stand at the top of a bump, with the tips and tails of the skis free from the snow. Slide forward slightly and use the phantom move to start a turn.

Details
Fig. a. Let the skis teeter on the top crest of the bump, then slide down by pulling your feet back under your body. Never push your feet forward, as this lowers the hips and makes you sit back!

Fig. b. Let the skis drop slowly into the trough of the mogul. Tip the free foot to the little toe side keeping your skis very close together. Maintain contact between the ski boots.

Fig. c. Keep the pole touching the mogul as long as possible. Use the pole to assist with balance as you move and turn into the hollow. Move the free side hand forward over the pole shaft to keep it up with the body's forward motion.

Summary
When you pick up the stance foot to tip it to the little toe side (making it the free foot), be aware that the foot and leg are tipped with the skis as parallel as possible. At times, tipping the free ski can separate the ski tips, especially when they are off the snow. Practice one bump at a time until you feel

c

comfortable going over bumps in both directions. Add a traverse approach, only turning on the perfectly formed bump.

Choose your terrain carefully. Some ski resorts have designated beginner bump runs. Although the terrain may be flatter, the bumps can be the ugliest on the mountain. Typically, if the bumps are not made fresh every morning they'll be tight, hard, and sharp because inexperienced bump skiers form them. It can be discouraging to ski a beginner bump run without success, but often these runs are more difficult than the expert bumps. Look for soft bumps that are round with shallow hollows between them.

Stand with your feet close together in the bumps. Top-notch mogul professionals ski with their feet tight together, moving them as one. The wide stance myth was unraveled in earlier chapters. Skiing with a wide stance creates "terminal intermediates" (credit for that phrase must go to *Breakthrough on Skis* author, Lito Tejada-Flores). Skiing with your feet apart in the bumps is a disaster.

Bullets
- Pick up free foot before moving
- Tip free foot
- Push off bump and pull feet back

Combining the principles of primary movements skiing that you have learned with judgment and quick reactions is bump skiing at any level. The key to bump skiing is keeping the stance ski on the ground. Even at the intermediate level, while trying to control speed, the ski tip may stick out from the top of the bump. Staying in contact at the break-over of bumps comes from pulling both feet under the body at the point of transition. Pull and hold both skis under the body at that point where there is least contact or ski friction, near the top of the bump.

Figure 10-2B, on the next page, gives an overview of the bump terrain where this sequence was shot. These bumps are ideal for learning because they allow for any size and range of turn. Although my turns are close to the fall line, they could easily be completed with a rounder arc for control. The pole plant is a crucial part of bump skiing. Timing of hand and arm movements will reflect the timing of turn transition. If you desire to keep with the pace of quick, tight bumps, increase pole plant action accordingly.

Be ready to pre-absorb the lip of the bump. Pre-absorbing is a term I use to describe what I do with my legs before the slope does it to me. Start flexing before you hit the lip of the bump for smooth transitions. Make a quick flexing movement to stay light over the next bump lip. If you are light at the lip there is no impact; no impact means you stay on the snow.

In Brief

Start your lifting and tipping movements before you arrive at the lip of the bump. Use the phantom move through the turn on the other side of the bump. Use flexing and lengthening actions of the legs to stay in contact with the snow. Use the pole plant to time balancing with stance leg changes.

Details, Photo 10-2A

Fig. a. Bend the stance ski by extending the stance leg. Strong loading of the ski is apparent by its bend. Tuck the free foot up and under the body close to the stance leg, but cleanly off the snow. Flex the elbow and wrist toward the shoulder to move the tip of the pole forward in preparation for the pole plant.

Fig. b. Plant the pole and transfer balance to the new stance foot well before your boots reach the edge of the bump. Use the pole plant to establish balance and to help transfer to the new stance foot. Relax both legs to avoid being thrown back on your heels when the skis hit the hollow of the bump.

Fig. c. Still using the pole, raise the free foot and tip it over to the little toe side. The arm on the new stance side prepares for the next pole plant by flexing the wrist and elbow to move the pole tip forward and to point it down the slope. Keep the free foot tucked under the hips. Use strong hip flexor contraction to bring the leg up. Allow the stance foot to float over the top of the lip; keep it from pressing against the lip at the break-over point.

Fig. d. Continue tipping the free foot while extending the stance leg to maintain contact with the snow. There should be no twisting or turning of the ski at this point. Make contact with the snow on the down side of the bump and the ski will change direction.

Fig. 10-2A. Subtle phantom move in bumps; first frames of fig. 10-2B.

Details, Photo 10-2B

Fig. e. This is the point of transition for another turn, like *figure a*; reach the pole tip so it is planted well out in front of the body. The pole plant supports the transfer and helps you to absorb the hollow. Extend both legs as you drop into the hollow and anticipate the lip of the coming mogul by flexing both legs to absorb.

Fig. f. Use the pole plant to stabilize the upper body. The new free foot is already off the snow and ready to tip to the little toe side. Again, it's the simple Phantom Move.

Fig. g. Concentrate to tip the free foot quickly. Tipping the free foot before the lip of the bump is critical. Keep the stance leg passive except for absorbing and stretching. Many skiers cross their tips and wash out the tails by actively turning the stance foot.

Summary

Be patient with the stance foot in the bumps. Notice in Photo 10-2A how soon my stance ski cuts the turn on the down side of the bump. If you turn or redirect it, your movement order is out of sequence. The stance ski must be engaged to ski the back side of the mogul. When you twist the ski before the back side of the bump, contact is lost, launching your skis into the bottom of the next hollow with no one on board. All bump movements in preparation for the next turn should be made before the hollow. Make sure you transfer to the stance leg in the hollow before the tips stick out into the air at the lip of the bump.

Perhaps to your surprise, bump turns use the same primary movements as the other turns in this book. The difference is the increased need to maintain snow contact through leg use. You need the hamstring flexing action to keep both feet under the hips. This is important to maintain sufficient fore/aft balance. Contracting the hamstrings so you can keep your feet under your body prevents the skis from shooting out from underneath you.

The position of the poles is also critical. The pole position is determined by hand and arm movements. Do your homework: develop hand discipline for bump skiing.

Bullets

- Flex legs to absorb in hollow
- Release and transfer before lip of bump
- Use pole to balance in transition

Fig. 10-2B. Linked turns in moguls

Advanced Bump Skiing

Aggressive bump skiing can take many forms. Having skied with and observed Bill Kerig, an eight year competitor on the Professional Mogul Tour, and other great skiers, I've come to the conclusion that there are varied approaches and philosophies to bumps. Bill is a special athlete who displays great quickness and strength. He worms his way down a bump run like a snake slithering through corn stalks. He uses tremendous strength and power to press his skis into the hollows and he absorbs the shocks of the oncoming bumps with his thighs. Bill takes a very direct, high-speed line, seemingly unperturbed by the size of bumps or steepness of slope. I probably have about two runs like that left in my body but I'd like to spread them over the next twenty years. Bill gave me some tips after I pestered him into coaching me on his technique. Now I am convinced that this is no way to ski bumps if you want to maintain the health of your knees and back. The pro bumper is a great athlete, but a very specialized bump skier. Still, much can be learned from their approach. Where do we go next for advice on aggressive bump skiing? I look to other skiers I admire, skiers who ski well in all conditions. Kim Reichhelm, for example, World Extreme Champion, is such a skier. I have known Kim since she was twelve years old. I coached her at Stratton Mountain, Vermont, when she was on her way to the US Ski Team. Kim skis everything well, especially ungroomed terrain and steep bumps. Kim uses bumps to turn around and control speed. She has great ability to judge terrain and remains in balance on even the steepest bump runs. Much of her skiing comes from her natural athletic ability, but Kim is a savvy skier who uses her feet and legs to maneuver her skis. Let's look at some of the techniques that these top skiers use to make aggressive bump skiing look so effortless.

Movement progression continues on following page

Previous:　*Phantom move in linked bumps*

10-3.　**Advanced bump skiing**

Next:　*Powder skiing*

a　　　　*b*

Fig. 10-3. Advanced mogul skiing

This series of photos was taken on a black run, at a "let them rock" speed. The foundation for bump skiing has been presented, but this section goes beyond relying on correct movement alone. To go after bumps in this manner, movements must already be intertwined with your natural reactions. It's similar to driving your car, when a dog jumps out into the road. It isn't necessary to give the "put your foot on the brake" command, it happens naturally. Skiing in the bad bumps is a combination of rehearsed technique and reactions. If every move is planned in advance, bump skiing becomes "posed". With no planning or practice, though, you can really let it hang out. Don't worry. A happy medium between posed and out of control exists, where practice and experience combine with spontaneity to create advanced bump skiing.

Details

Fig. a. Look forward and prepare before you are in the trough of the next bump. Visualize the movements you need to stay in touch with the snow. From repetition and rehearsal, it is instinctive now to release the stance foot and get the free foot on the snow.

Fig. b. Flex the legs and tip the free ski moving only the lower body. Your upper body, from shoulders to hips, is perfectly straight. Use the hamstring muscles to pull and hold the feet from jetting forward. Strong arm and hand discipline holds the body in balance; very little shoulder movement is needed.

Fig. c. Here the terrain drops off quickly, so extend your legs and continue to tip the free ski. Keep the feet under the body until you make contact, then relax and absorb with the legs.

c

Summary

Building a memory bank of positive bump experiences is important to further success in skiing bumps. Store positive experiences in your memory bank and don't stray too far into the unknown. It is preferable to ski two, possibly three good turns and then pull off the course, rather than force your way through a prolonged stint of bad turns that reinforce inefficient movements.

Unfortunately, I see the latter occurring in training everywhere I travel. Trainers and coaches alike are guilty of this overtraining of bad movements. I have seen it with instructors and young racers. They are subject to ingraining of incorrect movements by forced, repetitive training on difficult race courses or long, difficult runs. A purposeful, progressively challenging schedule of terrain and difficulty is the best method to building success. Ski on short but rewarding runs; begin by stopping after every bump to condition yourself to the next level of difficulty. I often refresh my attitude toward bumps by slowing down and studying the formation and pattern of the bumps. This exercise increases my awareness of potential routes through the peaks and troughs of the bump field ahead.

Bullets
- Release to stay ahead of terrain requirements
- Retract and flex the legs

Previous: *Advanced bump skiing*

10-4.   **Powder skiing**

Next: *Technique for kids*

Powder Skiing

This section is based on the assumption that all powder skiing is now done with some form of shaped or wide ski. This alone will boost your range on the fun dial by a factor of ten. There are few absolutes in skiing, but here is one you can take to the bank: don't ski powder again unless you have the new technology skis.

Early transfer is the key to unlocking the mysteries of all upper level skiing. Many people have talked about early transfer in other teaching systems but they haven't been successful in conveying the idea to the recreational or advanced skier. Even racers and top instructors are constantly baffled by how to achieve an early transfer.

Interestingly, there are other elite skiers who understand the value of the early transfer and teach it. About one and a half years ago, I met Rob and Eric DesLauriers of the Extreme Team through Bill Grout of *Skiing* magazine. We hit it off immediately, talking about Alaska and the great mountains and powder. What really piqued me was our discussion of their philosophy on ski technique. At their Extreme Camps, they use a primary movements approach to their instruction. They have different names for the movements, but fundamentally the approach is similar. The most prominent feature of their system is the emphasis on early transfer.

Let's explore early transfer. It is known in most circles as weight transfer. This term has always confused me. I've had skiers respond by admitting that they were on a weight loss program, but they hadn't yet accomplished transferring their extra weight. Transfer is introduced in many chapters and we call it either balance, support, stance transfer, or in most cases just transfer. These terms are appropriate and accurate to what you are doing or trying to do. Early transfer can be achieved if you are able to make the essential relaxing and releasing movements while still in the bottom of the turn. Your movements have to be quick enough to prepare you for the subsequent turn. The requirements of terrain, turn shape, and speed will put varying demands on your timing of relaxing and releasing movements. Releasing movements should lead into and connect to transferring, resulting in balance on the new stance foot. If balance is not established before you enter the arc of the next turn, you will be late and therefore rushed and skidding at the bottom of that turn. Incorrect movements are self-perpetuating. Consistency is never achieved unless the primary movements are used from the start of a turn.

Accurate use of primary movements becomes more critical at the upper levels of skiing. This is never more apparent than on a beautifully steep, deep powder run. Snowbird, Utah, comes to mind. You are the first at the top of the Gad Chutes, looking down at flawless, untracked powder. You feel exhilaration, anticipation, and… that gnawing, uncertain feeling in the pit of your stomach. The voice inside your head reminds you that your powder technique is suspect. The first few turns are okay, but speed builds and you can't keep up. "Turn those skis!" you think. Soon, your skis aim in different directions and you tumble gracelessly through the snow. It's just another reminder that you don't really have a strategy for powder.

To begin with, this thought process is sure to turn you into a big snow bundle rolling down the mountain. You need positive thoughts to produce positive actions. The correct thoughts need to be programmed into your mind, thoughts that produce top performance at or beyond your ability level.

It should be evident from the last section about skiing on expert terrain that your mental attitude is an integral part of skiing success. Let's keep it in perspective. You can have the best mental attitude in the world, but if you haven't developed the effective movements to complement it, it doesn't matter. I remember a book a number of years ago that had a Zen approach to skiing: a psychological approach to calm skiing. Get into yourself and know yourself to ski better. My experience from coaching racers tells me it is critical to have the right information in the memory bank before you let it go or let it out. If you are incorrectly programmed, you could be in for trouble, especially in a challenging situation. Using and knowing how to use positive mental strategies and tactics in conjunction with correct movement information is indeed powerful. Let's explore the movements that give confidence and develop a bulletproof powder skiing technique.

The first rule of primary movements for powder is to assume as narrow a stance as possible. This is easy for skiers who have been following the exercises in the book. Every movement should be done as if the skis were one. If you move the skis as one solid platform you have complete control all the time. One of the reasons that mono-skis are popular in parts of the country where they have big, heavy snow falls, is the wider surface which brings the monoski to the top of the powder easily and quickly. The new shaped skis have proven to be indispensable in powder because they provide this same characteristic.

The powder in this sequence is only six to eight inches deep, providing a visible demonstration of ski and foot use. The movements in deeper powder are exactly the same. This is an ideal depth for practicing powder skiing: six to eight inches with a solid, groomed base underneath.

Is there a difference in powder skiing technique compared to what we learned for carving and bumps? The answer is simple. Yes, the movements are the same, but minor differences need exploring. Let's start by describing the actions in the photo series. The turns leading up to this series were short and closely connected. One turn led quickly to the next, so active pole planting was central to keeping the movements connected.

Details

Fig. a. At the top of the turn, use the wrist to prepare for the next pole plant.

Fig. b. The elbow is bent and the pole tip is ready to be stuck in the snow. Start to relax both legs gradually, keeping tension in the muscles. Relaxing the legs does many things: it starts the release, moves the body in the next turn direction, and it lightens both skis, letting the ski tips come to the surface.

Fig. c. The pole plant action is the same as in the bumps. Plant it and leave it in the snow, but move that hand over the pole and forward to keep up with your forward motion. Stay centered on the skis, but low and flexed by relaxing the legs. This is similar to skiing over the top of a mogul and absorbing its lip. The action of relaxing the legs produces the same results as in the bumps: the skis get lighter. A lighter ski makes it easier to tip into the new turn. In transition, keep both skis equally pressured so they continue to perform as one.

Fig. d. Squeeze your feet, ankles, and knees close together at this point, causing the lateral tipping movements of both skis to act together. The leg squeeze immediately improves your powder skiing. The pressing action creates a balanced, solid body position and helps the skis to work in unison. Using the planted pole and arm for stability and balance, lighten or slightly pick up the free foot (skier's right) and make a phantom move. Allow no space to develop between the knees. The feet, ankles, and legs press together and assist in the tipping action of the phantom move. The tip of the free ski sometimes comes out of the snow when these movements are done quickly, but only for a moment, as both skis are again pressured evenly as the next turn begins.

Fig. e. The free foot leg continues to tip and flex, becoming shorter than the stance leg. The stance leg stretches out to stay in contact with the snow while the body reacts by moving to the inside of the arc. The free foot and ski must lead the tipping into the turn to stay out of the way. If the free foot doesn't tip early enough, it could cause the tips to cross. If you cross your tips while skiing it's because you are too active with the outside, downhill, stance ski. Notice that the arm on the free foot side is already in place leading the turn.

Fig. f. Both skis are bent into arcs and carve the snow cleanly. This turn is complete, so look ahead to the next one. Pole action prepares for the turn. The wrist and elbow are flexed back in preparation for the pole plant.

Fig. g. The legs have already started to relax, bringing the center of my body closer to and above my skis. The pole plant is never rushed.

Fig. h. Now the body is directly over the skis, the stance foot is totally released and out of the snow, and the legs are still pressed powerfully together - the first rule of powder skiing. The knees actually can be felt rubbing against each other when the pressing together is done correctly. The relaxing action of the legs reduces the resistance to gravity, causing my body to move toward its pull. I never tried to flatten my skis or move my knees toward the next turn. That all happens naturally. The Primary Movement system saves tremendous amounts of energy in powder skiing by eliminating the need to hop around and heave your skis into the next turn.

Summary

When you first start to ski powder it is sometimes difficult to get the right timing. I tell skiers to do some bouncing to get a sense of the bottoming ability of the skis. Bouncing moves the legs from flexion to extension, pushing the skis into the snow during extension, and bringing them back up to float during flexion. This action tells the skier how the skis respond to pressuring input. Try this

Fig. 10-4. Linked turns in powder snow

exercise during a straight run through the powder to get a feel for the snow's resistance. Then, take that action one step further. Start a slight turn by tipping the lightened free foot to the little toe side (phantom move) and extend the stance leg. Remember powder rule number one: press your legs together. You get some direction change but don't go too far; now flex both knees, especially the stance leg, to get you back to even pressure on the skis. You will come back to straight running. Next, switch stance legs, make a phantom move and the same turn happens in the other direction.

In powder there are two critical movements: the phantom move, to tip the skis from one side to the other, and the transferring movements from foot to foot. Think of the foot to foot movements as a game of distributing and equalizing your weight between the skis. You'll feel this as pressure on the bottom surfaces of the skis. If both skis are equally weighted they'll stay at the same level in the snow. If one gets more pressure, it starts to sink. Pressure is added to one ski by removing it from the other. As the less pressured ski is tipped to the desired angle it can be re-pressured, setting it into a corresponding carve and giving both skis the same action (as in *fig. f*). The skis should be unequally pressured only during the release into transition; otherwise, you should strive for equal pressure under each foot. As you become more sophisticated with pressure exchange, you will get closer to an ideal 50-50 split. If you can stay within 60-40 weight distribution when releasing and going into transition you will be very smooth. The pressure difference is due to one leg starting the relaxation to release before the other. Relax both at the same time to master powder skiing. More extreme weight bias toward a single foot is necessary for quick direction changes, but the duration of that distribution, at the transition, is very short.

You might have noticed that there has been little mention of forward and backward movements in the powder section. Many skiers are told to sit back in powder, but if you do you'll be stuck, your legs will burn, and your turns will suffer. There are several reasons why skiers might be told to sit back: first, to keep moving on flat terrain; second, to get the tips to come to the surface. The beauty of powder is the higher snow-to-ski friction, so with good technique you'll be able to ski on terrain that is steep. With shaped skis, the wider tip will come to the surface more readily than the submarines of old. The relaxing of the legs will encourage the skis to surface without sitting back. Only subtle movements are required to maintain fore/aft balance. I move slightly aft at the start of the turn by pressing on my heels as I extend the legs and tip the feet because I know that in the middle of the turn the skis will slow due to the resistance of the snow. At that point, my body will catch up to the skis. If you find that you are sitting down more than you like at the end of the turn, keep your feet tucked under your body as you start flexing, to keep your knees over your binding toe pieces. Make all of these adjustments slowly so that you don't end up too far forward all at once in powder, which leads to an over-the-handlebars tumble.

Skiing powder is a game of feeling push and float under the skis, not a matter of setting the edges into the snow. The idea is to tilt the ski bases at an angle to the snow surface. Snow compresses under the skis, forcing them to deflect and bend into a turn. The skis bend more and turn more sharply when they are pressured, therefore if you lengthen the stance leg in the upper part of the arc, the skis will change direction quickly using the forces provided by snow.

Powder skiing described here is for the advanced skier wanting to become expert. Terrain selection should start with moderate slopes for practice, but in powder you can ski more advanced terrain than normal. Shaped skis will immediately bring your skiing up a level. Using primary movements will bring it up two levels.

Bullets
- Flex to release
- Use even pressure to float skis
- Press legs together for stability

Chapter 11 - Technique for Kids

Kids Can Ski Great Too

The future of skiing is with our kids. This generation will start skiing on the shaped skis and revolutionize the sport. Sure, we go out and carve vicious arcs on our 143 cm rad carvers, but we do it with our prior experience of the sport. Now, kids can carve from the beginning of their skiing days. They will figure out how to use the skis and make it their sport, like nothing we ever conceived. Who has the responsibility to give kids correct basic movements, so they can use the new ski design, remains in question. I'm talking about movements that they won't have to unlearn later. Give them the correct tools to start with.

I teach kids. I teach my son. I always move kids away from the wedge. I've never taught it, nor have I referred to skis as "pizza wedges" or "French fries". If we treat kids with dignity and with an assumption of intelligence, the way we teach adults, they will show us how to move on shaped skis. Demonstrate simple concepts of movement that lead to success, and it will boost their self-esteem. Kids on shaped skis will reinvent the sport.

I teach kids primary movements with a slight altering of formality. I use more of a "to go over there, let's try this movement" approach. No lengthy explanations are needed or desired. There is very little terminology in the Primary Movements Teaching System. Look at the basic language: free foot, stance foot, and little-toe side. Anyone can relate to these concepts. I attach foot stickers to the tips of their skis, portraying the foot and the toes. The kids look at their ski tips for an immediate reminder of where and how to move. Tip the foot you want to turn toward. Tip the right foot to turn to the right. As soon as they understand these basic concepts and perform the movements, I remove the stickers. Have them feel the movements of their feet.

Young kids, aged four to six, can learn most of the language and movements indoors before they ever have to brave the elements on those bad days. Save many frustrating moments by introducing the plan in a friendly environment. Start the games indoors or out, but play with the balancing fundamentals. Use the basics as demonstrated at the beginning of the book without skis on.

I started skiing with my son, Harrison, when he was two, but his motor skills and understanding jumped a level when he was four. I skied with him about five days a season at that age. He's now eight, but even in this short time he has picked up the basic primary movements. Last season I skied with my friend Craig McNeil's children, Sean, who is seven, and Moira, who is five. I introduced them to the basic free foot and tipping ideas. In a matter of a few turns they demonstrated immediate understanding and increased skiing ability. They are skiing on shaped skis. Craig believes that the skis, although they were actually adult length, improved the kids' skiing almost immediately. With the introduction of primary movements both Sean and Moira were matching and skiing parallel within one run.

If kids are taught by any other method, their skiing development is hindered.

Shaped skis may not be effective for kids who are taught by traditional skiing methods. Let kids explore this great sport with their natural inquisitiveness. Free them from experiencing the structure of a stage by stage, dictatorial system. Let's look at some Primary Movements Teaching System approaches for kids in this chapter.

Fig. 11-1. Kids turn more easily on shaped skis. Harrison Harb, age 7, with Dad

In Brief

I never taught Harrison to twist or turn his stance foot. He started at four years old to ski balanced on one foot. Here he demonstrates part of the primary movement progression. It's a movement he never practices. We asked him to start in a wedge, pick up the free foot and tip it to its little toe side. He stands patiently on the stance foot and waits for it to turn because he knows that the shaped ski will react to the free foot movements.

Details

Fig. a. He starts in a wedge, because most kids are taught this first.

Fig. b. Lighten the free foot. Notice that immediately the skis come closer together. This is a natural balancing response. Skiers do not balance with their feet apart.

Fig. c. Tip the free foot to the little toe edge. The stance ski starts to carve.

Fig. d. Keep balancing. It doesn't matter if he places the free ski back on the snow. The point is that he is learning to balance on one ski. This will guide him in the right direction in his skiing life.

Fig. e. The free foot continues to perform the Phantom Move.

Fig. f. With continued tipping, the turn really starts to take shape. Put the ski back on the snow and lighten the other foot, swapping balance and support, to start the next turn.

Summary

All of the concepts we talked about in the early chapters apply to kids. Pick up the tail of the ski, and balance will shift toward the front and middle. Keep the arms and hands well out to the side and forward to increase balance awareness. Try movements with kids that teach body and balance awareness: have them spin in a circle without skis. Show them how to hold the arms out to the side away from the body while they spin. A dancer or gymnast will naturally perform this way. Apply it to their skiing movements. Use imagination to give them experience and comfort with movement. Traversing with the free foot light and tipping (Figure 11-3, on the following pages) is the same exercise we used early in the book. All the exercises apply beautifully to kids. With proper instruction, kids demonstrate exquisite adaptability and balance.

Bullets

- Pick up free foot
- Balance

Fig. 11-2. From a wedge, lift and tip the free foot. The shaped ski cuts a clean arc.

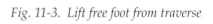

a

Fig. 11-3. Lift free foot from traverse

b

Balance on the stance foot, tip the free foot

The stance ski turns because it's angled to the snow

c

d

The shape of the ski takes Harrison on a ride to a round turn completion

(Facing page) Fig. 11-4. Putting primary movements to good use in powder

In Brief

Can't believe he's never skied in real powder until this season? This is his first day in powder. Naturally, he relies on balance and the primary movements. A little more practice and he could turn into a decent western-snow skier.

Details

Fig. a. Ready! Pick up or lighten the stance foot.

Fig. b. Relax the stance leg causing the knees to flex. Don't forget the pole plant!

Fig. c. Pressure the skis evenly in the transition while the free foot tips to the little toe edge.

Fig. d. Started tipping the free foot in *figure c* and it worked, so keep it going.

Fig. e. Was a little late with the release of the stance foot, but it's catching up.

Fig. f. Now I'm back in shape, the free foot is pulled over and doing the tipping thing.

Fig. g. Having a great time. This powder stuff is OK, Dad!

Summary

Harrison skis about two weeks a season with me on his Colorado visits, and last winter we skied in the East for two days. Harrison skis on 123 cm Elan junior shaped skis. They are still a little too long for him, but next year there will be shaped skis for kids starting at 90 cm. He loves their turning characteristics, the deep arcs that they carve. They made a big a difference in his skiing. He is skiing with much more confidence since switching from his traditional kid skis. The shaped skis give him superior balancing ability between turns, and once they start into the turn the edges carve as with adult skis. He tips the free foot to start carving, therefore the ski performs as it was designed.

Bullets

- Release the old stance foot, bring it close, and tip it before engaging the new stance foot

Fig. 11-5. Harrison's on the primary movements track - tip the free foot and ride!

Chapter 12 -Alignment

Harb Skier Alignment Centers

Information is power

Information is power, especially when making purchasing decisions. An understanding of alignment will change how you purchase ski lessons, foot beds, boots, and shaped skis. In this chapter, we cover what to buy, and why to buy it. This is required reading if you want to enjoy skiing like you never thought possible, save money and time, and prevent frustration.

The Alignment Centers that I started have created a wealth of knowledge about skiers, skiing, and ski equipment. In the past four seasons, my personal understanding of the needs of skiers and how to meet them has grown enormously. I'm not talking about subtle refinements in technique. I mean helping skiers make educated decisions and effective choices - decisions that influence your attitudes about the sport, your performance, and your well being. I have developed this information through testing, observing, adapting, and judging the results. Modifications include just about everything you can do to ski boots, including grinding inside and out, re-riveting, straightening, and adding straps, in order to change design properties slightly or completely. The program has shown that some of the most popular boots are inappropriate for certain skiers. Just as boot fit characteristics must match the skier's needs, so must the boot's functional and skiing properties match your lower body anatomy. Proper equipment selection can prevent the extensive tailoring sessions mentioned

before   *after*

Fig. 12-1. Bowlegged skier, before and after alignment

above. Equipment selected for your individual anatomical and skeletal structure maximizes ski performance. Combined with accurate coaching, you add enormous development power to your skiing.

> *"The greatest impact on my skiing, besides the Harb Alignment process itself, was the recommendation to switch from narrow-waisted skis to wide-waisted skis. This change dramatically enhanced my stability, as well as my ability to initiate a carved turn."*
>   *Don Glazer, D.P.M., F.A.C.F.S.   Board Certified, America Board of Podiatric Surgery*

These services are offered through certified "Harb Skier Alignment Technicians" and are tied to specially trained instructors that teach the Primary Movements Teaching System. Harb Alignment technicians and instructors are professionally trained to establish with you a complete skiing development program, comprising equipment tailoring and personalized, movement-based instruction. Confusion is eliminated from equipment integration, alignment, and skiing methods; it's virtually a one-stop skier empowerment center.

Would you like to know why certain boots help your turns and others do not? Some of the variables include cuff design, ramp angle, and forward lean. What's right for you - a narrow or wide-waisted shaped ski? If you were armed with this information, could you make better purchasing decisions? I think so. Obtain the information to make educated decisions about equipment that considers your body and movement capabilities. Trained alignment center staff make the connection between your equipment and the way you ski and learn to ski. Don't take years to become an expert. No one has time to waste learning to ski, especially the wrong way. Want to make your learning curve to parallel as fast as teenagers taking to snowboarding? Through these systems your improvements on snow will last, and will continue. The Harb Skier Alignment Center takes the responsibility for your skiing satisfaction, and creates the changes in your skiing that you want. You just go out and enjoy the skiing.

In the past four years, though the fundamentals remain constant, I have worked to develop and improve the technical approach to alignment. My staff and I are able to refine the program because we work with so many skiers - more than twelve hundred this past season. We are developing innovative techniques to streamline the alignment process and make it available to more skiers through more ski schools and ski shops.

After twenty-five years as a ski coach and teacher, I am amazed by the biomechanical understanding of skiing that has developed, but am frustrated by its limited acceptance. I am hopeful that this understanding will be more widely held in the future. Since the mid-Seventies I have been grinding boots for racers to help them ski better. The results were extremely favorable, because I was working with racers who trained daily throughout the winter. A motivated and persistent coach can always determine and implement the correct modifications. Every measurement and change can be tested on snow, in races or time trials. With the skiing public, there isn't the luxury of skiing every day. As with the racers, though, on-snow testing for all skiers should be an integral part of the assessment. Evaluations on snow prior to and after adjustments are essential to create major improvements. That's why I developed the Harb Expert Skiing Balance Evaluation (HESBE) sessions.

Since the first Alignment Lab developed four years ago as the precursor to the Harb Skier Alignment Systems, my staff and I have worked with thousands of skiers. Each assessment adds to the accuracy of the techniques and procedures that result in significant skier improvement. I emphasize that these are tangible, quantifiable improvements, not pat-on-the-back, temporary, feel good changes. Our programs offer tools and training to instructors that help them make a difference with students. In this chapter, I will introduce these procedures and tell you how to take advantage of my information for your skiing, boot selection, foot bed needs, ski purchases, and ski instruction.

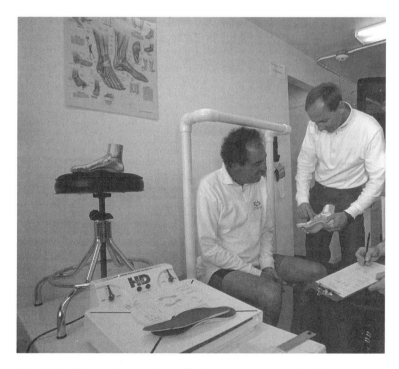

Fig. 12-2. Discussing results of indoor assessment with client

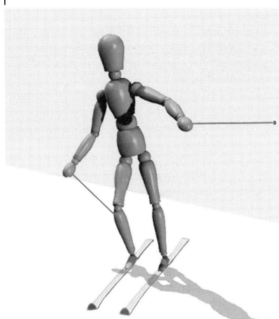

Fig. 12-3. Typical bowlegged skier　　　　　　*Fig. 12-4. Typical knock-kneed skier*

Alignment: The Structural Foundation for Balance

Four years ago, I made the statement that "Boot alignment is the single most important performance issue in skiing." I believed that then, but now, after thousands of alignment evaluations, I believe that alignment is optimized through a complete system, not just with the boots. This system includes the following components, equal in importance:

1. Movement instruction
2. Foot bed design
3. Boot alignment
4. Boot selection
5. Skis, lifters, tuning, and binding compatibility

Harb's Theorem on Skiing Improvement:
Correct, efficient movements, complemented by correct alignment and tailored equipment selection, produce expert skiers rapidly.

Corollaries:
A. Poor alignment limits the benefit of good instruction.
B. Poor instruction eliminates the benefit of correct alignment.

Unfortunately, these truths are not self-evident!

Many of our clients consider the Alignment Center as their last chance. They feel used, worn out, angry, frustrated, and ready to give up skiing. I have determined some of the common causes of these feelings:

• Spending a lot of money on equipment doesn't guarantee that you'll get the right equipment. You may end up with the wrong ski boot model or brand that contributes to and causes alignment problems.

> *"The ability to stay balanced over my skis and to execute controlled, carved turns has been a longtime goal. Through the alignment process and the movement instruction I received with Harb Skier Alignment Systems, this goal is a reality."*
> Jim Pitcock, MD

• The wrong ski boot for a skier's leg anatomy or skiing movements can add to skiing problems. For example, a knock-kneed skier in "rotary boots" will experience greatly reduced edging ability. Similarly, bowlegged skiers with stiff, "lateral boots" will struggle needlessly. More discussion of boot characteristics follows later in this chapter.

• Improper foot bed design or materials can cause locked ankles and feet. Foot beds with the following characteristics can be harmful or of no value: overcorrected or inappropriately corrected, incorrectly supported or overly rigid, or soft and unsupported. Foot beds such as these offer no clinical value. These types of foot beds are made every day in the ski industry.

• Contradictory movement information: incorrect movement information nullifies your efforts to be aligned and properly equipped.

The ski industry has yet to ask the question, "Why are people frustrated with skiing?" The answer is simple: the different components of skiing that determine skiing performance are difficult to integrate for the benefit of the consumer.

Solutions and Answers

What is the solution that will speed your improvement? Work with an Alignment Center that has instructors who understand the way you ski and your equipment needs. Do the research: find a ski school that is trained in the Primary Movements Teaching System or contact a Harb Skier Alignment Center.

Training in biomechanics and kinesiology is critical for ski instructors and technicians if they are to provide accurate information. The Harb Skier Alignment Centers are raising the standard, providing value for skiers at a level heretofore unknown in the ski industry.

We have hundreds of stories from skiers who were frustrated and on the verge of quitting. A couple whom I met when I was coaching at the Snow Country Ski Schools comes vividly to mind. The director of the schools came to me early on the first evening, before the group meeting, and said,

"Harald, I have two people who insist that they have to be in your group." John explained that they had read my articles about skiing and alignment and were certain that I was the answer to their struggles. They had been through almost every available program, foot beds, new boots, canting, and lessons, yet they still had major problems. They were ready to quit. They were ready to hear that they were not athletic enough to be skiers. Not one to turn down a challenge, I agreed that it would be best if I skied with this couple. As is often the case, I had the pleasure of meeting two wonderful people who had a sincere desire to ski with more ease and control. Suzy had skied for years, but was still on green terrain making turns with a wide wedge and very little parallel action of the skis. Before we even started on snow I checked their equipment and started the process of alignment.

To make a long story longer, over a period of twelve months we stayed in touch, skied together, made equipment changes, and worked on the technique presented in this book. After only the second session they went from being timid skiers, barely bringing the skis parallel from a wedge, to making parallel turns on blue terrain. It has been three years since we first met. Now Suzy skis on black diamond terrain making carved, parallel turns.

What had gone wrong in Suzy's previous efforts at alignment? As with most skiers who have problems with boot fit, boot performance, and alignment, too many steps and people were involved with the original equipment selection and adjustment process. It is the industry norm to select boots based on skier ability and fit. Rarely is a skier's lower body anatomy and alignment matched to a boot that will minimize leg alignment and skiing movement problems. Testing through the alignment process demonstrates that a skier, measured in two different brands of boots, can vary in alignment by as much as two degrees in static measurement. This is due to different lateral and rotary characteristics of each boot. The situation is made worse on snow. If you are knock-kneed by one degree, which is common, and you are put in a boot that aligns your leg one degree further toward knock-kneed, you are two degrees knock-kneed and your skiing will suffer tremendously. The ski shop boot fitter may be doing his or her best, putting you in a popular brand that is comfortable on your foot, but it's without knowledge of what the boot will do to your skiing. A different boot that has the right characteristics for your alignment will reduce, and could even eliminate, the need for alignment modifications. In our example, it could bring you one degree in the correct direction, solving your alignment problems.

In Suzy's case, she had a boot that seemed to fit but didn't help her alignment, so she went to the next person in the process for canting. This accomplished, she headed out for a lesson with an instructor who was unaware of alignment or reasons for her alignment changes. So where was she? She had a great boot - but it was opposite to her alignment needs; she was canted - but her lesson didn't take advantage of it.

I raced bicycles for years, and bought what I thought was the best frame. I then bought the best components to build up the bike. That's just what I ended up with, the best components. Until I fit the frame and adjusted the components to my body proportions, I wasted tremendous time and energy overcoming incorrect fit. This analogy is completely appropriate for skiing. Individual components of alignment don't add up to satisfactory solutions unless they are coordinated and optimized to improve your skiing. Save your time and money, and avoid frustration - look for the integrated system to meet your alignment needs. Skiing is too rewarding to be performed at a subpar level, especially now that you can get it correct from the beginning. The integrated system includes the following components:

- Ski instructors with biomechanics training
- Primary Movements Teaching System
- Ski shop connected to the Alignment program offering individual equipment tailoring and selection
- Harb Skier Alignment Center Program

There is one aspect of the alignment process to keep in mind: the ultimate goal of the process is to improve your skiing. If the alignment proceeds without an evaluation of your skiing, chances are that it will not meet your expectations. Indoor alignment without a skiing evaluation is inaccurate, because the dynamic situation on snow is different from the indoor, static measurements.

A complete alignment process can avoid these problems. It is worth the effort. You will be rewarded with pleasurable skiing every time you go on the mountain.

Stance Width

We teach skiers in the PMTS Direct Parallel method to ski with their feet relatively close together. We often teach intermediate skiers to narrow their stance. The reasons are clear and logical. A narrower stance allows for many different movements unavailable in a wide stance. Movements of expert skiers are closely related to standing with balance over and on the skis. The expert skier freely allows the hips and mass around the middle of the body (center of mass or center of gravity) to travel from one side of the skis to the other. Intermediate skiers and skiers who have reached a plateau in their progress do not have that ability and don't know how to break through to the next level. A wide stance that lowers the body into an inflexible, locked hip position does not allow for movement of the center of gravity from one side to the other. I often hear the argument that racers ski with a wide stance. This is just not comparable to a learning skier and it is not true. First, a racer skis at speeds that are not available to the recreational skier. Second, the racer actually skis with the feet vertically separated, but laterally close: in the turn the inside feet almost touches the outside leg.

In PMTS Direct Parallel skiing, we also use the narrow stance and the pulling of the feet close together for awareness and balancing exercises. This does not mean we recommend that the skier keep the boots touching at all times. It is, however, very educational to ski with boots touching, as it makes skiers aware of how their bodies move and balance over their skis. A functional stance width is four to six inches apart, for speeds up to twenty miles per hour on intermediate slopes. On expert slopes where you need higher edge angles the feet are vertically separated, by as much as a foot or more, while they are still laterally separated by four to six inches. Hence the inside boot will be almost touching the shin or the knee of the outside leg. (This will be discussed further in the section on Carving in *Expert Skier 2*).

Kinetic Chain

When the integration of foot bed, alignment, equipment, and movement is achieved we can use subconscious reactions or "passive dynamics" as a foundation for balanced skiing. Passive indicates without conscious effort. Passive dynamics means that once an action, such as a ski turn, is started correctly, the action will continue successfully without conscious additional efforts; the body performs subtle refining movements subconsciously. Ongoing, active, gross balancing movements are a compensation for misalignment or poor movement habits. Skiing down the mountain with the exhilarating sensations of wind in the face, swooping turns, and carving skis, unfettered by thoughts of imbalance or control, is what we strive for. You can experience these sensations when your body's kinetic chain is functional.

The kinetic chain is a complex version of "foot bone connected to the leg bone," and so on. Your body behaves much like a steel link chain. If you shake one end of the chain, the links starting at the shaking end will react and transmit the shaking to the rest of the chain. The motion continues along the chain until the energy is absorbed or dissipated. The body maintains an upright, balanced position and is like this chain but much more sophisticated. One end of the chain reacts when the other end is moved. If the base of that chain is nonfunctional or locked, the chain requires bigger shakes to compensate for the stiff links. Now, think of a chain that has links that get progressively larger, starting with small ones on one end and ending with large ones at the other. If you shake the small end, the motion doesn't get very far up the chain before the energy is absorbed. Shake the large links, though, and the movements transfer to and disrupt the small links quickly and violently. The body reacts similarly in many ways. The large links represent the upper body, while the small links are the foot and ankle. If you use the upper body you will create large movements. Many skiers must use their upper bodies to make skiing movements. This causes constant disruption of balance to the smaller links. The foot and ankle are the small, fine-tuning joints with tremendous balancing and adjusting capabilities. If configured properly, they allow balance to be controlled from the base up. The upper body doesn't have to make large balancing adjustments, and it can absorb the movements of the lower leg without losing stability. All great skiers have stable upper bodies, and perform their skiing and balancing starting at the foot.

When the kinetic chain in skiing is functional, it allows the foot and ankle to be the primary control center. The links in the body's chain are held together by ligaments, but are controlled by muscles and tendons. The muscles work on either side of the joints, providing opposing contractions to stabilize the joints. As one muscle shortens, the muscle on the other side of the joint must lengthen. The body is most efficient in balancing when the muscles that control a joint's movement are able to work together or cooperate in controlling the joint. This action of cooperation is called co-contraction. Effective co-contraction is essential if the kinetic chain is to be helpful with skiing.

Co-contraction is the ability for opposing muscle pairs to act on a joint in a cooperative way, maintaining joint stability.

Try the following exercise to experience balance and co-contraction. In shoes or bare feet, stand on one foot. Watch the actions of the ankle and foot - they move or wobble to maintain balance. The rest of the body just gets in line to take advantage of this balancing act. It requires very little movement at the top end. This is a functional kinetic chain. Note how the center of the body (belly button area) shifted when you moved from the two-footed to the one-footed stance. The center of your mass, which is somewhere around your belly button, must stay aligned vertically over your base of support. In the two-footed stance, it lines up in between your feet. Glance down to see this position.

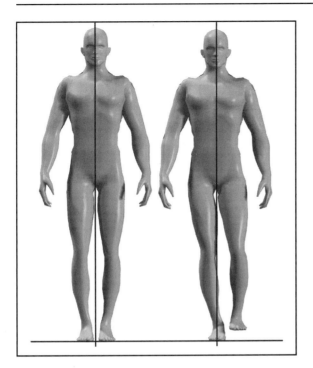 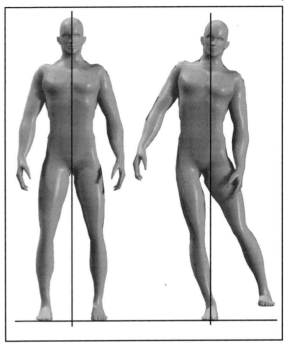

Fig. 12-5. One-footed balance in narrow stance;
Little adjustment needed to create balance

Fig. 12-6. One-footed balance in wide stance;
Gross upper-body adjustment needed for balance

When you stand on one foot, the center of your mass moves over to line up above your stance foot. This experiment demonstrates the simple dynamics taking place with your body during balancing activities. The same happens on skis when you pick up a foot to balance.

What if the ankle and foot were not able to perform the activities of co-contraction for some reason? The next set of muscles at the hip joint must perform these duties. These muscles are larger and control large joints. They don't have the fine-tuning or sensing ability of the ankle co-contractors, therefore the upper body must participate in balancing. Stability is diminished. The arms start flailing around, the head and shoulders move. I see these same movements everyday on the slopes with skiers who use their adductor and upper thigh muscles to drive ski turns. This is an extremely inefficient way to ski, requiring more energy and resulting in fatigue earlier in the skiing day. Much of the blame for this kind of skiing can be attributed to locked co-contractor muscles around the ankle. A muscle imbalance due to ankle conditions such as excessive pronation or supination is often the cause. Proper foot beds and boots can help these conditions. Incorrect foot beds can force a skier to use inefficient, large muscle balancing movements. What if a skier with an overcorrected, rigid foot bed took a lesson? The instructor, without prior knowledge of the foot beds in the student's boots, is destined to fail.

The Ankle

Over the years, if you were standing on the side of the slope while I was coaching or training instructors, you probably heard me make statements to the effect of:

- The most important part of skiing happens inside the ski boot.
- The essence of skiing is hidden by the ski boot.
- The ankle is the most important joint in skiing.
- Therefore, use the foot and ankle to lay the ski on edge.

I think you get the idea. The use, function, and knowledge of the ankle and foot in skiing are important. So what about the ankle makes it so important?

The ankle, at the base of the kinetic chain, has more ability to control balance than any joint in the body. The ankle provides both fore/aft and lateral balancing movements. The foundation of skiing control is connected movements at the bottom of the kinetic chain. Can you ski without ankle balance or co-contraction? Yes, you can ski, but without complete ankle function you can never achieve the finesse, control, and edging precision required to become a powerful, elegant, competent skier.

The rest of the story requires evaluating ankle function with the ski boot. Since not all ankles are made the same, and few skiers know what their ankles need, proper ankle capability and function must be analyzed and measured by a competent technician. The ankle actually has two joints. Ankle function in the lateral movement plane depends on the range of motion in the lower joint of the ankle, called the subtalar joint. The foot also contributes to eversion if the ankle is locked or has limited movement. Fore/aft movement happens at the upper joint in the ankle, the talocrural joint. I will bring up the importance of this joint later in the discussion.

The ability to move the ankle inside the ski boot is necessary for proper tilting, edging and balancing. Although movement is limited in a ski boot, the slightest lateral movements apply a load to the ski boot wall and establish stability for the entire body. The boot is the only point where we can create leverage in skiing. Force is applied to the side of the boot with ankle and foot movements. This pressure against the boot side stabilizes the ski edge and body at the same time. It is the connection between upper and lower body. The mass of the upper body can be controlled by the small movements at the ankle. If the upper body initiates movement, the upper body mass is set into motion and is no longer controllable from the base. The body then moves without precision.

The smaller muscles that control ankle function offer far superior precision for edging than do the gross motor muscles higher in the body such as the rotators of the femur and trunk. The other way to create angles or tilting is by pressing against or retracting from the snow surface, with leg extension or retraction. This is a much slower and less accurate method, but can be very effective when used in conjunction with tipping the feet and ankles.

Increasing Ankle Function

Skiing foot beds and orthotics produced by the medical fields (podiatry, pedorthy) generally emphasize controlling or eliminating excessive foot and ankle motion – pronation. This understanding for making ski foot beds was transferred from running and walking mechanics of people with excessive pronation. This is why we mostly see oversupported and rigid foot beds in ski boots. These devices lock the ankle and foot and reduce the skier's finesse and edging ability.

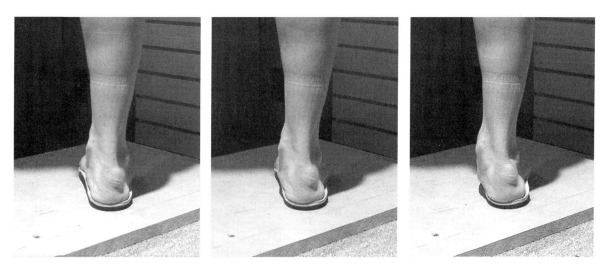

Fig. 12-7. Demonstrated here is the movement of the ankle and foot necessary for the ankle to put pressure onto the side wall of the ski boot.

In our years of skier analysis, we have discovered that rigid, high-arched feet are also non-ideal for skiing. Very little effort has been put into analyzing and diagnosing the limitations of rigid feet and ankles. In skiing, the functional limitations of a rigid foot can be more severe than of the pronating foot. The objective for enhancing function of the rigid or supinated foot is to increase the limited range of motion. Therefore there are no special foot beds designed for this condition. We have discovered various methods using a foot bed in combination with a specially modified boot board to enhance rigid foot function.

Foot Bed Design and Construction

Harb Skier Alignment's approach to custom foot bed design incorporates the correct amount of freedom to allow natural balancing movements of the joints. The system builds foot beds that provide balancing and fine edge controlling abilities. Edge control is far superior if it originates at the ankle rather than higher in the kinetic chain. Lateral movement ability and external leg alignment are more critical than ever with shaped skis. A rigid foot bed device inhibits the kinetic chain. Foot bed design should enhance balance. This is called a dynamic foot bed balancing system. An accommodative foot bed that enhances balancing function of the small muscles of the foot and ankle is the goal. A foot bed made with materials that accommodate and support alignment, yet are pliable enough to allow natural articulation of the foot and ankle, is ideal.

The foot bed is potentially the glue that holds the alignment system together. A properly adjusted foot bed refines balancing ability for the final connection to the ski boot and therefore the skis' edges.

An expert foot bed maker is an artist and a technician. The technical part is the understanding of how and why measurements are taken. The artistic part is taking the measurements and transforming them into the end product. A well-trained foot bed maker who understands all the measurements and

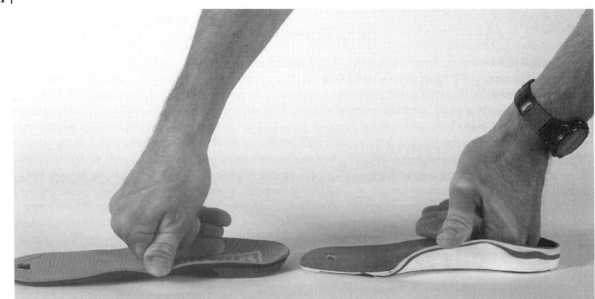

Fig. 12-8. Footbed comparison, flexible vs. rigid

uses all the components available to create a satisfactory end product is truly your skiing ally. The foot bed must match the skier's performance needs, boot properties, and foot. The craft is manufacturing and producing correct heel angle and combining materials to allow foot balance. It's difficult for a customer to know if all was done correctly. Foot beds come out looking like an upside down mold of the bottom of your foot. Will it really make a difference? Any and every foot bed provides a new feel and takes up room in the boot, so yes, there is a difference. Most skiers never know if the different feel is making them a different and better skier.

How, then, can you be sure a foot bed will make you a better skier? A complete foot analysis and measurement process is necessary for successful foot bed design. Here are some critical measurements that must be taken and incorporated to achieve a quality foot bed.

Calcaneal angle: the angle from vertical of a line that bisects the heel.

Accommodation built into the foot bed should produce the appropriate heel angle for your stance. The technician measures this angle and than builds accommodative angles into the heel of the foot bed to make the ankle functional in ranges of motion to either side. If this is not done, co-contraction cannot be achieved, and thus the kinetic chain is broken.

Range of subtalar motion: the travel of the ankle's lower joint (subtalar) in side to side movement.

Although some reasonable foot beds can be made without this measurement, the true foot bed artist would never do without it. This range helps determine the neutral position of the ankle, in which the kinetic chain is strongest. It also determines the tightness or looseness of the ankle joint in this movement range. This information helps in selecting the density or rigidity of materials needed to build appropriate stability.

Forefoot varus or valgus: the amount of twist or torsion of the forefoot, or simply the ball of the foot, relative to the hindfoot, or heel.

This is observed from behind, while holding the ankle joint in neutral (called neutral subtalar alignment). If the big toe side of the forefoot is raised or is higher than the little toe side, there is a twist in the foot known as forefoot varus. This twist can contribute to pronation of the hindfoot and internal rotation of the tibia and femur. Filling in some of the space under the big toe side of the foot (to about 70% of the measured angle) supports the forefoot and lines it up relative to the heel. Accommodating forefoot varus can reduce pronation and is beneficial in tracking (tracking is extremely important, and is described later in more detail). Most foot bed systems do not take the forefoot into account, but doing so can make an enormous difference in establishing the kinetic chain and providing positive edge feel. If you have never felt the ski edge along the whole foot, even though you have a foot bed, you may need support for the forefoot.

Fig.12-9. Calcaneal angle

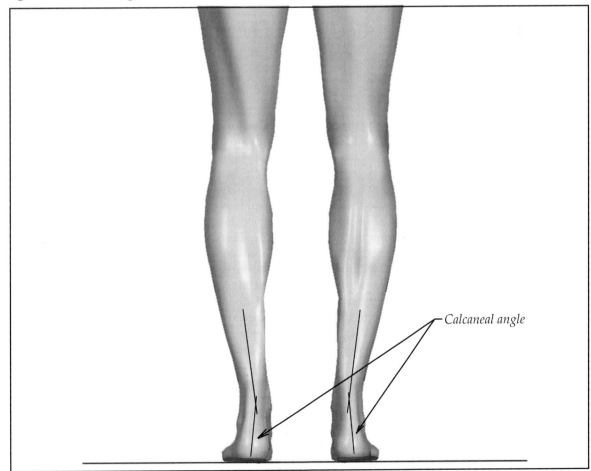

Dorsiflexion: the range of motion in your ankle when you lift your toes toward your knee.

This measurement is taken with the foot unweighted. Ten degrees is usually sufficient. A limitation in this range of motion is present in about twenty percent of skiers, and it can have serious consequences. If your heel lifts up or your toes jam into the front of the boot when you flex, or you are always "sitting back," you may have a limited range of dorsiflexion. The appropriate ski boot is crucial for the skier with limited dorsiflexion. A ski boot with a vertical shaft and a stiff forward flex can be very beneficial in this situation, positioning the ankle within its range of motion. (More on boots and fore/aft adjustments comes later in this chapter.)

Tracking: the direction your knees move as you flex your legs

Tracking is one of the most important considerations in determining foot bed and alignment adjustments. It is done first in bare feet to determine foot bed accommodations. A quick home assessment of your own tracking is simple. Stand with your feet parallel and at a comfortable width apart (when your toes are pointed straight ahead and the feet are parallel, you may feel as though you are standing with the feet toed in). Face a full-length mirror and flex your knees, keeping your feet planted firmly. Watch the center of the knee track forward as it flexes over your toes. Ideally, each knee's center should move straight forward and parallel to the other knee as you flex. You may have a tracking problem if your knees move apart toward the outside of the feet, or flex inward or touch as you bend them. Tracking problems have different degrees of severity but they can be helped by a well-made foot bed. Tracking is a major part of the overall alignment evaluation. A final determination of foot bed design is not made until all the other measurements discussed are considered. The bare foot evaluation can include preliminary adjustments with rubber wedges placed under the foot to assess potential accommodations.

Pronators

A true pronating foot and ankle has excessive movement or motion. As a quick self-check, compare your foot when it is unweighted and weighted. Sit in a chair and put your foot lightly on the floor. In this lightly-weighted condition, most feet will exhibit an arch. When you stand on the foot, does the arch go flat and does the ankle bone move to the big toe side? If so, then your foot is pronating under load. In skiing this causes lack or loss of edge hold. This condition is correctable, but it requires a well made foot bed tailored exactly to your needs. The foot bed design must take into consideration your weight, range of motion in the subtalar joint, and nominal calcaneal angle. These must all be measured and accommodation built into the foot bed. Very good results have been found with this approach for recreational skiers as well as top racers. The common incorrect way which we often see in skier foot beds is to construct a footbed with a hard, rigid, high arch.

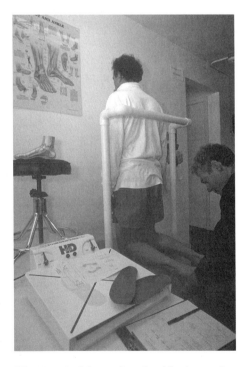

Fig. 12-10. Measuring dorsiflexion and forefoot/hindfoot relationship

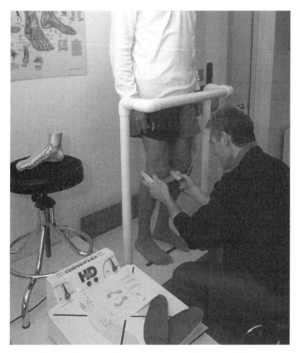

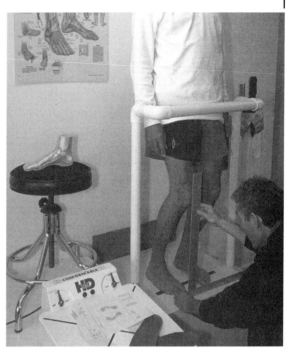

Fig. 12-11. Measuring the center of mass of the top of the tibia

Fig. 12-12. Measuring alignment of knee to foot

Technicians and instructors trained with Harb Ski Systems can usually see signs of a pronating foot from on-snow balancing exercises. The general posture of a skier with pronating feet is detectable and distinguishable, often from a skier's stance and movement.

Supinators

If excess mobility impedes the progress of the pronator, then a lack of mobility is the handicap for the supinator. Just as the pronator's foot is already totally collapsed into the boot and therefore has no ability to exert pressure on the side of the boot, the supinator can try to apply pressure, but cannot because the ankle does not move sufficiently to the side to exert pressure on the boot's side. Through various methods (foot bed design and boot board modification), we have been able to give the supinator movement of the ankle to the side, when initiated by the proper muscles.

Functionally Flat Feet

It is not unusual that we find people with totally functional flat feet who are restricted from their proper movements by poorly designed foot beds. Many foot bed technicians are misled by the flat foot. A flat foot looks like it is a pronated foot when the subject is standing. There is no visible arch and the inside ankle bone often is highly obvious or visible. So far, this sounds like a pronating foot to me. However, if you apply the unweighted to weighted comparison as described for the pronating foot, you'll find a difference. With little or no weight on the functionally flat foot, it still exhibits no arch. The flat foot can often move and pressure the side of the ski boot if nothing is in its way, namely an artificial, high, rigid, arch in an unsuitable foot bed. Many customers come into our alignment center with an oversupported foot bed for a flat foot. This locks the flat foot, preventing proper use of the foot for skiing. Many skiers with flat feet discard their foot beds because they hurt. A foot bed should not hurt at any time. If you have a foot bed that hurts, you have an improper foot bed.

In-boot Tracking

In-boot alignment is done similarly to the bare foot tracking assessment. The boot has considerable influence on the tracking and nominal leg alignment. Skiers wear shorts and stand in ski boots on a flat, hard, level surface for this evaluation. The first step is to mark the center of mass of the tibia at the top of the lower leg. In general, this mark falls on the tibial tuberosity, the vertical ridge on the shinbone below the kneecap. In cases with severe tibial torsion (a twist along the length of the shinbone), the tibial tuberosity is ignored as it provides an incorrect and misleading measurement. An experienced technician can easily evaluate this condition.

A carpenter's framing square (a large right angle) is used to drop a vertical line from the knee mark to the boot. This measures nominal alignment. The skier then flexes the legs while keeping the boots planted firmly. The top of the square moves with the knee mark while the base of the square stays in contact with the floor surface. This allows the technician to see and measure tracking, changes in the knee position from the starting position to the fully flexed stance.

Many alignment shops use a plumb bob, a pointed weight on a string. A plumb bob is very difficult to use. Any time the knee moves, the weighted pointer at the bottom of the string moves. This is difficult to control. The plumb bob must be held and its movement stopped before a measurement can be taken. The other inconsistency of the plumb bob measuring procedure is at the point of origin. The string must be held against the skin on the knee while the client is moving. This position often changes as the technician tries to hold the string and stabilize the weighted end.

Other devices exist to measure alignment, many of which allow the foot to tip from side to side as the skier stands. You must stand on a hard, level surface to obtain consistent measurements. The skier's dynamic physiology on a moving or tilting measuring device produces inconsistent and inconclusive results. The tilting device compromises tracking measurements yielding a less than complete measurement approach.

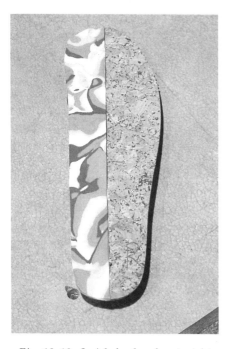

Fig. 12-13. Swirled colored material is soft enough so that the foot can create a better angle in the boot by dropping into the softer material.

Fitting the foot bed to the boot:

Almost every ski boot has a "boot board," a removable platform inside the shell on which the skier stands. They come in all shapes. The boot board embodies the boot designer's philosophy for comfort in initial fit or performance. The foot bed must be designed with consideration of the boot board. Some ski boot

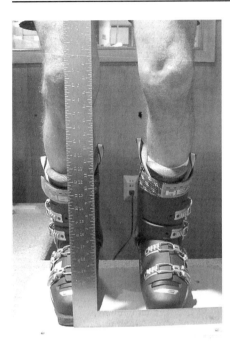

Fig. 12-14. Neutral alignment as measured in ski boot

companies have up to three degrees of boot board angle at the heel that can affect the function of the foot bed. The intended foot bed design can be magnified or negated by the boot board. Foot bed technicians will often grind the boot board so that the foot bed acts as it did on the level design surface.

Modifying Alignment

A skier's nominal alignment, measured as described in the In-boot Tracking section above, determines how far we bring the skier in the initial adjustments with angled alignment strips. Through my research I discovered that there is no single ideal alignment, no one point on the boot sole where the tibial mark should drop. All skiers are different in build, strength, and nominal alignment. Therefore their final alignments vary according to individual needs. Several factors affect the amount of alignment material I use, including the type of boot (rotary or lateral), level of skier, type of ski, length of leg, and amount of lifter under the binding. The Marker binding company makes the shims or alignment materials we use, but they can be modified to fit other bindings. The shims are angled, thick on one side and thin on the other. They come in half-degree increments and are the width of the binding. They are installed directly under the binding and can hardly be seen when installed. The shims tip the boot sole relative to the ski in order to bring the skier to a more functional alignment. New for 2000 is Dalbello's "SGS" boot, a patented design which allows the boot upper to pivot along the sole in order to modify alignment. This boot will eliminate the need for alignment on the ski. Read more about it in the Boot section of this chapter.

The effect of the shim (or boot tipping) on alignment can be confusing. Many people believe that the technician is moving the knee sideways, in or out from a vertical line to the center of the boot sole. This misconception is easy to understand given that instructors often tell their students to move the knees into the hill. Knees don't move sideways. When the knee appears to move laterally, the upper leg or femur is actually rotating in the hip joint. Try the following experiment. Stand with your weight more toward your right side. Using the left leg in this test, move your knee medially, toward the right knee. Notice how the left upper thigh rotates clockwise in the hip joint when viewed from above. The opposite is true when the knee is moved away from the body centerline: the femur rotates counterclockwise.

Observe Figure 12-20 (p. 204): this skier's knees are touching. It appears that she has her knees too far to the center, too close to each other. In actuality, her femurs are internally rotated. She has very little control over this situation because it is her natural stance. When she stands on a flat surface for a static measurement, both knees line up to the inside of the big toes. Skiers who demonstrate this alignment are called knock-kneed. With this alignment, the skier will never make a parallel carved turn. However, knock-kneed skiers can be aligned properly and given the correct movements to overcome this alignment problem.

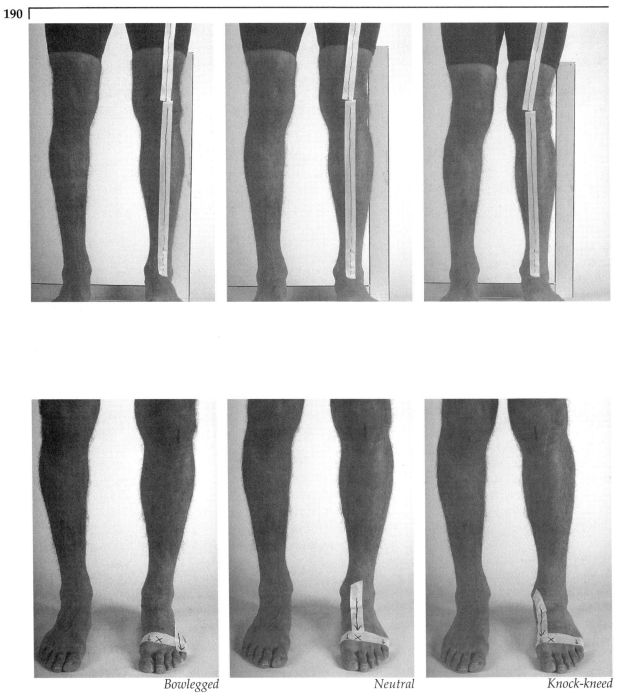

| Bowlegged | Neutral | Knock-kneed |

Fig. 12-15. Three types of alignment - upper to lower leg relationship (top); pressure concentration across foot (bottom)

Fig. 12-16. Filming the alignment assessment maneuvers on the hill

The tables in the On-snow Analysis section of this chapter describe the kind of movements misaligned skiers make in the three critical components of the turn - release, transfer, and engage. Reading the table may answer some questions about your skiing. You may find that you fit some of the descriptions of the misaligned skier. If so, you're not alone. We have found that ninety percent of skiers can benefit from some alignment changes.

Again, using the left leg as an example, rotating the femur to move your knee as much as 1/4 of an inch right (medially) or left (laterally) can have a profound influence on your balance, edging, and ski controlling abilities. It can change your way of skiing. Done without proper understanding, this can be detrimental to your skiing. Every time a shimming adjustment is made, the angle of the boot sole to the surface changes. This changes where you stand over the foot: it can put your weight toward the outside edge of the foot (little toe side) or the inside edge (big toe side). These adjustments need to be integrated with all the other elements of the alignment procedure, including the foot bed and movement patterns. The influence of each change must be considered through the process so they are complementary.

As mentioned earlier, contrary to popular understanding there is no single ideal position in which to align the knee. The skier's on-snow movements must determine the final positioning or alignment. In general, we try to bring most skiers closer to the center of the boot sole, but this "spot" does not apply to all skiers or all boots. Boot selection and boot design will be discussed further in the section on lateral and rotary boots. Skier strength, limb length, and experience are important considerations that we use to determine a balanced position for each individual. Ultimately, a skilled instructor or technician is helpful in determining optimal alignment.

On-snow Analysis (Harb Expert Skiing Balance Evaluation)

The first step in the alignment process is to ski through a specialized, on-snow balance assessment. The indoor measurement process alone does not adequately assess a skier's alignment needs. How the skier balances and moves on skis is crucial to the success of the complete alignment program. Our on-snow balance assessment demonstrates the skier's functional alignment and balancing ability. Difficulty balancing can stem from alignment problems, improper foot support, or incorrect movement. Incorrect movement instruction can cause a skier to move in a manner that mimics or exacerbates alignment problems.

If I could adjust all skiers to 1/4 of an inch to the inside of the centerline of a ski boot using the indoor static evaluation, alignment would be easy. The factors that influence your skiing go beyond static canting adjustments. Muscle strength, flexibility, skier ability, lower leg curvature, leg length, ski design, and boot selection all influence your movements and balance. No single measurement can

Fig. 12-17. Analyzing the assessment maneuvers

offer a complete solution. Analyzing skier balance and movements on snow provides the complete evaluation to optimize skier ability.

Balancing Exercises

The skiing assessment uses several exercises to test balance: one-footed balancing in a straight run on flat terrain, a traverse on one foot, phantom moves, and turns. We are not concerned that you make your five best turns, or that you demonstrate a certain technique. We want to see the total balancing picture. This procedure is recorded on video for a before and after comparison. It is important for the evaluator to understand the student's movement background and motivation during this process. An understanding of skier goals must be agreed upon between the evaluator and the skier. Understanding motivation focuses the direction of the process toward meeting expectations and therefore ensures a successful outcome.

The following tables describe some of the alignment-based movement patterns demonstrated by skiers in the assessment maneuvers and in the three components of linked turns - release, transfer, and engage.

Maneuver	Knock-Kneed	Correctly Aligned	Bowlegged
On gentle terrain, one-footed straight run.	Femur of stance leg rotates to inside, shoulders lean to outside. Knees may pinch together. Lifted ski often points across stance ski. Stance ski veers to inside or skids.	Subtle balancing movements occur at the stance foot. The rest of the body remains quiet. The lifted ski aims straight ahead. The stance ski runs straight.	1) Hips move toward little toe edge of stance foot. The lifted leg or arm on that side are held away from the body. OR 2) The hips are moved to the outside of the stance foot, then the stance foot is twisted to make the ski tail skid.
Edged, straight-line traverse on stance foot.	Femur of stance leg rotates in, shoulders tilt downhill. Knees may pinch together with lifted ski pointed across stance ski. Stance ski hooks uphill or skids gently sideways.	Subtle balancing occurs at the stance foot. The lifted ski points straight ahead. The stance ski leaves a straight line in the snow.	Stance leg remains long and straight. Shoulders may lean uphill. Arms typically involved in maintaining balance. Stance ski may skid, or wobble on and off its edge.
On very gentle terrain, phantom move from straight run. The free foot is lifted off the snow and tipped to its little toe edge. The ski tip can touch the snow.	It's difficult to balance on one foot - the femur rotates in and the ski veers. When the free foot is tipped, it's impossible to balance and the free foot is set back down. The knees pinch together.	It's easy to balance on one foot. When the free foot is tipped, the stance ski tips gently onto its edge and creates an arc. Body remains quiet, stable, and balanced.	1) When the free foot is tipped, the stance ski runs straight. The shoulders may twist into the turn, accompanied by leaning the body. OR 2) The hips are lowered and the stance thigh is twisted into a turn. The stance ski tail skids out.
Garland: two-footed release using foot tipping, and engagement with phantom move.	*Release:* Skis don't release simultaneously, knock-kneed look apparent. Downhill ski keeps skidding with knee over big toe edge, uphill ski catches. *Engage:* Difficult or impossible to tip uphill ski to little toe edge. Downhill ski tail washes out. Body may turn and look uphill.	*Release:* Skis move simultaneously and to same degree using subtle foot and ankle movements. Shins remain parallel. *Engage:* Skier can lift and tip free foot. One-footed balance is established. Stance ski rolls onto big toe edge and gradually curves uphill.	*Release:* Skis don't release together. Gap between knees apparent. Shoulders often twist. *Engage:* The downhill ski rails and goes straight, or it skids. The shoulders are twisted and leaned uphill to "encourage" the ski to turn uphill.

Turn Component	Knock-Kneed	Correctly Aligned	Bowlegged
Release	It's difficult to flatten both skis to the snow simultaneously to get off the old edges. Approaching release, the skis skid farther than the desired line because there isn't enough edge grip. The knees are the focal point of movement - the skier tries to move the knee in to edge. Often, the skis are both on their big toe edges. A push-off from the downhill ski is often required to get the body moving into the new turn.	The skis are tipped to the same angle approaching release, and the stance ski is gripping the snow. Release occurs via controlled tipping of both feet. Gravity and momentum pull the skier into the new turn. The upper body remains balanced and quiet.	This skier must make skiing movements with the upper body and upper legs. Pushing off the uphill ski leans the body into the turn as well as extending the body away from the skis. This creates a release. Typically, the extension is accompanied by a shoulder and hip twist. Some skiers flatten and pivot or float the flat skis far enough to the side that they are angled to the upper body, and then let them grip the snow.

Turn Component	Knock-Kneed	Correctly Aligned	Bowlegged
Transfer	Since the release is not accomplished by tipping movements of the feet, the skier must push off the downhill ski while it is still on edge in order to transfer balance to the uphill ski. The uphill ski is often wedged relative to the downhill ski, as both skis are on their big toe edges. Weight transfer is rarely achieved high enough in the turn arc to make a round turn and control speed. The skier must aim the new downhill ski into the fall line with a leg twist, which worsens the situation - it skids the tail and pushes the ski away from the body, making it impossible to balance on the new stance foot.	Transfer of balance is accomplished by relaxing the stance leg, and lightening and tipping the free foot.	Weight transfer is not achieved until the second half of the turn, after the skis have crossed the fall line. In the upper half of the arc, the skis are flat and brushing or skidding across the snow, and the skier stands on both skis. At the point where the transfer is made, a large twisting force from the legs or upper body is required to continue the turn and prevent the skis from railing or chattering. When accomplished through strong leg twisting, this sometimes results in a knock-kneed position. Floating or flattening the skis until the upper body contributes to edging is common.

Turn Component	Knock-Kneed	Correctly Aligned	Bowlegged
Engage	The knee of the stance leg is driven into the slope as hard as possible to try to achieve edge grip. The body's reaction to this movement creates oversteering of the skis. Oversteering creates instability and becomes dangerous with speed and on difficult terrain. The ski tail feels loose and slippery, and it plows the snow until it's sideways across the hill. The upper body follows the skis and sometimes faces back up the hill. Some skiers use strong "counter" - turning the pelvis in the opposite direction to the turn - to prevent overturning the femur of the stance leg.	Tipping the lightened free foot facilitates movement of the body to the inside of the turn, thus edging the stance ski. Balance on the stance foot is easy to maintain because the stance foot remains a stable platform while the free foot tips to adjust edging.	Engaging is accomplished by leaning the upper body into the slope. The load on the skis and body is high as the edges start gripping. Chatter or bouncing of the skis is common at the bottom of the turn. Grip control is achieved by large flexing movements of the legs and body to absorb the shock of the edge bite.

Boots

Boots are the most important part of the ski equipment performance package. Skis may be more exciting, giving pure action feedback, but boots can make or break a skier. The most important feature in boot selection has always been fit. Then come adjustments, also known as "bells and whistles", and of course, the price. Recently, some performance features have been presented as skiing enhancements. Anti-vibration devices, cuff canting adjusters, and double power straps fall into this category. Even more recently, carving boots made their debut, perhaps to keep up with the carving skis. And I thought I could carve before carving boots came along! Let's take a step by step approach to unraveling some of the confusion and claims that abound in this endless maze of products. What should skiers know about ski boots before they buy?

Fit

It goes without saying that fit must be the first consideration when buying new boots. Modern boots are mostly overlap shells that have excellent fit characteristics. Overlap shells have buckles on the front, usually two over the foot and two up by the shin. The upper and lower portions of the boot each "wrap" around the foot and ankle, with one end of the wrap tucking under the other. Feet come in many widths and volumes, therefore boot manufacturers produce a variety of models to accommodate a wide variety of feet. If you have a narrow foot, make sure that the boot manufacturer or fitter isn't filling in the excess space in a wide shell with extra foam padding. The fitter should take the liner out of the shell as part of the fitting process. Length and width can be evaluated this way. Place your foot in the shell without the liner. To determine proper length, move your foot forward until a toe just touches the front of the boot. Reach down and place your index finger behind your heel. If there is room for one finger behind the heel but no more, it is a very tight fit. If you have room for two fingers pressed together it is a comfortable fit. If there is room for three fingers behind your heel, it is a luxurious fit. This finger test gives you a ballpark estimate. The general rule in fitting is that the boot should feel snug on your foot. Almost every skier I have fitted responds with, "Wow! This is too tight!" After several days of wearing, boots do stretch an average of one half size.

Test the width the same way as the length. Put your foot in the shell without the liner. Move the forefoot back and forth across the width of the boot to get a sense of how much movement you have. If you have minimal clearance, perhaps an eighth of an inch on each side of your foot, the boot will be too tight. If you have half an inch on either side, the boot will be too wide. Unfortunately, you can't get your finger into the boot that far to test the space. Use your judgment. This test should help in the overall decision, but try not to base your purchase on one measurement alone. Most boot fitters will measure foot width and length before you put your foot in the boot. The fitter will also know which boot models tend to accommodate the different foot dimensions. These guidelines will help you get a better sense of basic fit considerations. One thing to beware of, if the boot fitter has to put extra padding and foam into a new boot to make it fit, you are compromising your performance before you start.

A third check is to try on the liner without the shell. Your toes should not be curled or appear as bumps at the front of the liner. The toe box bulges from your toes appearing on its surface mean pain. In most cases, skiers pick boots that are too large, not too small. If your foot is in the liner and you have extra wiggle room, the boot will likely end up being too large, especially if the width is also generous.

Performance fit or racer fit

The basic rule here is the tighter the better, within reason. Two fingers or less behind the heel is a common starting point for performance skiers. Aftermarket liners like Zipfit and Conformable are often used to get a tighter fit around the ankle and heel. Some aftermarket liners are reinforced with plastic that can be molded to the inside contours of the shell, adding lateral stiffness to a boot. Racers often size their shells too small (one finger behind the heel) and require grinding of the inside to get the extra toe room. These extreme fitting procedures are not necessary or desirable for most skiers.

Rotary or Lateral Boots: Which is for you?

Lateral and Rotary are performance designations that refer to the manner in which a boot transmits edging or tipping efforts from the leg to the ski. Design and material-related factors make different boot models feel and act differently when a skier tries to tip the boot onto an edge. The difference in performance thus makes certain models more appropriate for certain skiers or alignments. Again, the consumer should know about the performance characteristics of various boots in order to make an educated purchase. In a 1993 article in *Snow Country* magazine, I wrote about boot performance and introduced for the first time the concept of Rotary, Lateral, and Neutral boots. It sparked considerable interest as well as controversy because for the first time it described valid performance characteristics of ski boots.

Lateral Boots

Lateral boots are designed to transfer tipping energy directly to the ski, without introducing any pivoting motion. They are preferred by racers, performance skiers, experts, and shaped ski skiers. Lateral boots are a must for knock-kneed skiers. Lateral boots are designed to offer strong, rigid, lateral stability without any lateral deflection or bending. All tipping energy is directly transferred to the ski when the boot sides don't flex. These boots need very little tipping energy to bring the skis on edge, as tipping energy is transferred to the ski rather than dissipated in a flexing cuff. Lateral boots support the leg in balancing, directing tracking in a straight line or even to the outside. The beefed up cuff sides allow little twisting of the lower leg. These characteristics are beneficial to the knock-kneed skier because lateral stiffness prevents lower leg rotation and inward knee tracking. Lateral boots are excellent carving boots.

Design features:

Lateral boots have riveted sides and the cuffs are tipped to the outside. The lower part of the shell extends well up into the upper part of the boot, often sticking out above the cuff. The forward lean angle of the cuff shaft is fairly upright (close to vertical) and the forward flex is controlled to prevent excessive knee drive that results in pivoting on the ball of the foot.

Lateral boots are not always the most costly. Some boot companies offer very strong lateral power in their mid-price range models.

Rotary Boots

A rotary boot is one that allows the lower leg to rotate internally before the boot applies lateral tipping forces to the ski. Rotary boots make it easy to steer or twist the skis into turns. Their design characteristics allow the cuff to move with the legs as they are turning and tracking. Skiers who have bowed legs will find that some rotary boots help to bring their alignment closer to neutral. A rotary boot can make it easier for the bowlegged skier to roll the ski on edge. Try to be cautious, though, because some of these boots are so flexible in tracking that it is difficult to achieve consistent measurements or alignment.

Design features:

Some rotary boots feature cutouts in the shell near the flexing points. The cuff hinges and rivet positions generally allow the cuff to flex to the inside. Often, the lower part of the shell stops below the top of the cuff. Others build forward lean into the lower boot and upper cuff.

Any boot with significant forward lean or that allows the cuff to flex freely without a progressive resistance or a stop will cause the ski tails to wash out. When trying on boots, take the lean angle into consideration. While you walk around in the boots, try to stand straight. Try to stand and move for an extended period with the top buckle closed. Do you find that you are constantly leaning on the tongue? Do your legs start to burn? If you have large calves, forward lean will often force your legs excessively forward making the aforementioned situations worse. Do you feel a lot of pressure on the ball of your foot? Identify these situations before you purchase boots; the conditions that are minor annoyances in the shop will become major irritants on the slopes. A boot with steep ramp and forward lean angles often leaves the boot technician with few modification options other than major grinding. If you discover after skiing in the boot that the lean is too much, it may be difficult to make changes.

Experimentation and subsequent on-snow testing with before/after video has demonstrated that rotary boots are detrimental to knock-kneed skiers. These already compromised skiers get worse due to ski boot design. Ski boots that we define as rotary can accentuate medial knee alignment in static measurement by as much as two degrees over that measured in a lateral boot. This becomes apparent on snow when knock-kneed skiers in rotary boots try to tip laterally to an edge but never find grip. The rotary qualities of the boot absorb the attempts to tip by allowing the leg and boot to twist. The motion of the boot cuff combined with forward lean and

Fig. 12-18. Lateral boots have riveted sides with cuffs tipped to the outside. Rotary boots have cuffs flexed to the inside.

a raised heel prevent the knock-kneed skier from achieving edge grip. A skier who has a hard time holding an edge despite ski tuning, or who can't seem to make shaped skis carve, may be in a boot that isn't transferring lateral tipping energy to the ski. At least one prominent boot company values these features; I ask why? Be aware that if you rely on accurate information you will get the boot that suits your needs. Take the guesswork out of boot purchase. Go to a ski shop that has an alignment professional.

Forward lean and ramp angle:

The cuff of alpine ski boots (the portion that wraps around your leg) slants or leans forward; when the boot is fastened around the leg, the shin will extend at a forward angle out of the boot, rather than vertically. The angle at which the cuff aims forward of vertical is called forward lean. The forward lean of ski boots varies from one model to another, and from one manufacturer to another.

Forward lean contributes to the transfer of rotational (twisting) energy to the ski. Therefore, most lateral boots have reduced forward lean. Many boots today have some forward flex control. When a skier flexes the knee forward, a large range of motion can transfer excessive pressure to the ball of the foot. If the skier tries to tip the ski on edge while pressure is on the ball of the foot and the shin is pressed forward into the boot tongue, the ski tail will skid because it is light. The tipping action in this bent leg situation generates strong twisting forces through the femur's leverage and the adductor muscles of the inner thigh.

Ramp angle is also important to consider in boot selection. What is ramp angle? The boot board, in the bottom of the boot underneath the liner, supports the foot inside the boot and has a slope built into its length. The back part, where the heel sits, is higher than the front part, where the ball of the foot and toes sit. The angle created by this difference in height is called ramp angle. Ramp angle, like forward lean, varies from one boot model to another, and from one manufacturer to another. Dalbello's Carvex series boots offer adjustable ramp and forward lean, simplifying the process of achieving good fore/aft balance.

This angle might sound insignificant, but it has a profound effect on your fore/aft balance and on your ability to tip the ski on edge, especially when coupled with forward lean. The tongue of the boot was not meant to be a shin rest. Imagine that you are wearing cowboy boots. Don't you stand on your heels to take the pressure off the ball of the foot and the quad muscles? A high ramp angle coupled with strong forward lean forces an overly bent leg position, a surefire recipe for quad fatigue. It many cases this also causes the skier to maintain a low, overflexed hip position, draining leg energy. This can be measured and corrected through the use of a force plate - a device that measures the distribution of pressure under the boot soles. The solution is often to reduce the heel height and bring the cuff closer to vertical. This straightens the legs and takes pressure off the ball of the foot, redistributing pressure along the length of the foot. The force plate is a tool used to confirm that boot modifications produce desired results. Force plate results demonstrate that heel lifts are inappropriately used for most skiers because lifts require the hips to counterbalance by assuming a lowered and backward position. All these indoor measurements and modifications are tested on-snow and recorded by before/after video to ensure skier improvements.

Some prominent, top of the line ski boots have considerable forward lean and ramp angles, enough to cause rotary actions in turns. Although a boot may have some of the properties described earlier as lateral attributes, like stiff, high sides and rivets, forward lean and ramp angles can outweigh the lateral design to still produce rotary actions. Many boot gurus will explain that it is a stiff, racing boot, believing it therefore to have strong lateral and edging qualities. This is not the case if high lean and ramp angles are present. Most boot manufacturers advertise the racing appeal and World Cup results of their boots. The boots used on the World Cup might look like the retail boots, but they are completely different from boots that most manufacturers sell to the public. World Cup race boots are different designs made from different molds and plastic. The point here is that you shouldn't be fooled into believing that a boot is quick to the edge or laterally strong based on the company's racing results, because you're not buying the product that is winning. My own feelings on this subject are strong. I believe that some of the boot company claims are stretching the truth. My boots are not advertised as boots that are used by World Cup racers. I don't need them to be. I need them to work, and they do.

Cuff adjustment

First, cuff adjustment is not canting, nor is it a substitute for alignment. Many boot manufacturers use this term incorrectly. Canting started years ago and was the method of aligning skiers' boot soles by placing wedges of different degrees under the boot. Cuff adjusters change the cuff's lateral tilt angle, and allow the cuff to conform to the angle of the lower leg. If you were to look from behind at the lower legs and feet of several individuals, you'd see that on average, the lower part of the shins aims slightly outwards, but that there is some variation in that angle amongst the individuals. The cuff of a ski boot, despite the padding of the liner, is stiff, tall, and close fitting. If its angle is significantly different from the skier's leg angles, it can be uncomfortable, and can have a negative influence on the skier's alignment and lateral balance. A cuff adjustment allows the cuff to be tilted laterally, to conform to the leg angle, while still fastening firmly so that the boot's edging ability is not diminished.

Not all boots have cuff adjustment capability. This doesn't mean they aren't performance boots or top of the line models. In fact, some of the most successful racing boots don't have cuff adjustment capability. These boots are designed to produce quick lateral response, therefore the upper cuff is fixed rigidly to the lower shell. These boots fall into the lateral category in our performance rating.

Many boots do have adjustable cuffs. This means there is a device of some kind that allows the upper part of the boot to move relative to the lower. The device is usually located near the anklebone on the outside of the shell. It is loosened to enable the upper part of the boot, called the cuff, to move. When loose, the cuff can tilt slightly from side to side, bringing the inner or medial side of the cuff either closer to or further from the leg. Lowering the lateral side (outside) of the cuff moves the inner side of the cuff toward the leg. Raising it moves the inner cuff away from the leg. The majority of skiers can adjust the cuff by first loosening the screws that hold the cuff in a fixed position, then buckling the boots and flexing forward vigorously five or six times. The cuff will center itself to your tracking and leg angle. Tighten the screws to fix the cuff in that position. A friend can be of assistance here. Further cuff adjustments can be extremely beneficial to skiers who have more specialized alignment needs. These adjustments should be made after a certified alignment technician has done an evaluation.

In cases requiring more specialized adjustment, moving the inner side of the cuff (between the legs) closer to the leg (lowering the outside of the cuff) makes the boot quicker to the edge, thus it becomes more of a lateral boot. Moving the cuff farther away from the inner side of the leg (raising the outside) allows the shin to travel farther before edging, so the boot behaves more like a rotary boot.

Boots for Optimizing Alignment

Equipment that optimizes your balance, both lateral and fore/aft, is a key to your skiing pleasure and progress. Skiers are diverse in build, strength, and natural alignment, and many skiers are asymmetrical from one side to the other. Thus, equipment that adjusts for and accommodates a range of angles can simplify optimizing your balance. Several models of Dalbello ski boots provide these adjustments. We are finding favorable results in using these boots with our clients. Not only do the boots fit well, but they improve balance and alignment.

Our on-snow assessments have shown that the combination of ramp angle and forward lean has a strong influence on your fore/aft balance: the "position" you stand in, your range of balance, and your ability to maintain balance. Fore/aft balance is primarily determined by your body proportions: shin, thigh, and torso lengths. If the boots you buy don't have adjustments for forward lean or ramp angle you are limited to the position the boot determines for you. A boot with fixed angles can be fine if you have the right proportions. If you don't, however, the boot with fixed angles may be difficult to modify in order to improve your balance, especially if has a high ramp angle and steep forward lean to begin with. It is easier to add ramp angle and forward lean angle with padding than it is to grind boot boards, and remove and reattach cuffs. The best situation for optimizing your fore/aft balance is to choose a boot with adjustable ramp and forward lean angles, as well as flex control.

Carvex series

Dalbello's Carvex series boots provide these adjustments, thus they can meet the balance needs of skiers with a wider range of body proportions. Even if you can't visit a certified alignment technician, you can experiment on your own with the boot adjustments to see which settings you prefer. Dalbello provides an adjustment chart with their Carvex series boots. The chart guides you to the proper settings for the adjustments based on body proportions. It is easy to use and understand, and it provides an initial setting for all skiers. Fine-tuning can even be done on the slopes.

The ramp angle is adjusted by a mechanism that moves the heel of the boot board. Using a hex wrench, the small screw (see arrow) can be turned in either direction, raising or lowering the heel position, thus increasing or decreasing ramp angle. The forward lean is adjusted by a mechanism on the upper rear portion of the boot cuff which adjusts the forward angle of the cuff. On certain models it is a thumbscrew; here, it is adjusted with a hex wrench (see arrow). By turning the screw, the cuff leans more forward (increasing forward lean), or stands more upright (decreasing forward lean).

The stiffness of a ski boot - its resistance as you press against the tongue - varies with the design of the boot, the material from which it's made, and how tightly it's buckled. A flex adjustment allows the boot's stiffness to be modified independently of its fit. This is beneficial for numerous reasons.

Fig. 12-19. This boot has lateral edging characteristics and an upright stance, determined by the combination of the cuff rivet placement, forward lean angle, and boot board ramp angle.

Skiers come in many bodyweights for the same size foot - a slim, willowy skier may want a softer boot, while a sturdy, muscular skier may require a stiffer boot for adequate support. Skier preference varies greatly - some skiers like a stiff boot, while others prefer a larger range of flexion. Ski boots, made of plastic, change stiffness as a result of outdoor temperature. When the plastic is warm, as on a spring day or in the shop, the boots will be quite soft - they will flex more easily and farther. When the plastic is cold, on an early winter morning, the boots will be much stiffer, and will flex less. A flex adjustment allows the same boot to provide adequate, pleasing performance and a functional range of flexion to a variety of skiers, under a variety of conditions.

The flex adjustment on the Dalbello Carvex series boots is a mechanical device on the back of the boot cuff. A lever, large enough to be operated with your gloves on, is switched by hand between three settings: Carve, Walk, and Ski. In the Walk setting, the boot can hinge freely both forward and rearward. In the Carve setting, the boot can free-hinge forward, but is prevented from straightening beyond the forward lean setting. In the Ski setting, the boot is mechanically locked at its forward lean setting, thus it is the stiffest.

Skis

Finally, we arrive at the skis. Whether you call them shaped skis, parabolics, super sidecuts, or hourglass skis, everyone is excited about the new ski designs. (To be accurate, there is only one parabolic brand ski, made by Elan. Elan produced one of the first skis to appear in the shaped ski revolution. Remember that the term parabolic only applies to Elan skis.) Now, almost every ski company is making several models of shaped skis. Shaped ski buying can be challenging, even for the trained professional. We will approach the subject by dividing the skis into categories based on their performance relative to alignment needs. Almost all skiers, whether professionals, part-timers or avid vacationers, can benefit from alignment through ski selection. Some may need it less than others, but all can benefit. Professionals who have skied all their lives benefit from alignment. Even former Olympic skier Andy Mill came through our program and made positive changes to his skiing. Once you know the general shape of skis that will complement your alignment and enhance your skiing, testing or reading any of the magazine tests should lead you to a ski you can enjoy.

Shaped Skis Improve Alignment and Skiing

Shaped skis, if correctly selected, can decrease your need for alignment. The wrong shaped ski, one that doesn't match your leg structure, can amplify your misalignment. This will certainly contribute to a negative first impression of shaped skis. You could end up being a shaped ski skeptic. This would truly be unfortunate, because there is a shaped ski for every skier. I believe that shaped skis are far superior to anything yet produced in skiing history. If you try a shaped ski that minimizes your alignment deficiencies, your skiing will go up a level or two and you will feel like a new skier. The manner in which a shaped ski tips on edge is largely influenced by its width under foot. This waist width thus becomes the parameter that determines alignment suitability. Once you know your alignment tendencies, you can tailor your search through the shaped ski racks to those models that will help you ski better.

Narrow-waisted shaped skis

I worked with many groups of skiers last winter, and we tried various combinations of skis. We wanted to determine their impact on improvement. Interesting results brought forth new theories about how the designs affected skiers. I vividly remember one dramatic example. The weakest member of the class was feeling embarrassed because he couldn't keep up. He was especially frustrated to appear inept before the group because he was a Phys. Ed. teacher - an athlete! He was obviously awkward and very bowlegged. The instructor (trained with alignment procedures) brought him to the alignment center for an assessment. The results demonstrated what she had suspected from his skiing: bowed legs, by about three degrees, which is a significant amount. The instant, quick fix: put two-degree shims under each boot. This brought his legs straighter and improved knee tracking, but he was still severely bowed. The next step: a pair of narrow-waisted shaped skis. The waist on a narrow ski disappears under the boot sole. When you look down at your feet, all you see is boot, no ski. Typical ski boot soles are 70 mm wide, wider then the skis. The narrow shaped skis have waists around 62 mm wide. Since the boots hang over the side of the skis they are easy to tip. It's like an inverted pyramid, wide on top, narrow underneath.

Bowlegged skiers like our PE teacher have difficulty moving their legs over the inside (big toe) edge because their knees line up over the little toe side of the boots. Tipping the ski, therefore, requires more lateral effort. The technician pulled out narrow-waisted skis and installed the alignment strips. Within one run down the mountain, with the new equipment and alignment combination, our skier was skiing as well as the best skiers in the group. Although this was an informal test it was obvious to everyone present that the skier improved measurably, instantly. Most companies make narrow-waisted shaped skis. If you have bowed legs and tend to have difficulty getting the skis to roll on edge, try some narrow-waisted shaped skis.

Wide-waisted shaped skis

Wide-waisted shaped skis are very popular and they suit many skiers. They are particularly helpful for the knock-kneed skier. Remember Suzy, who had trouble making all of her ski equipment components work to complement her movements? Knock-kneed skiers' knees line up over their big toes or even further inside. On a narrow-waisted ski, the knock-kneed skier's knees can line up inside the ski's big toe edge. This is an unstable position. Balancing on one foot becomes impossible, the ski just tips over. The skier gets stuck on the inside edges, and the skis won't arc. The skier in Figure 12-15 demonstrates this knock-kneed position. A wider-waisted ski is like an outrigger canoe. The wide-waisted ski comes to an effective edge angle with less lateral motion of the leg, so the ski bites and arcs before the knee moves too far to the inside. Skis with waists wider than 70 mm actually stick out farther than the side of the boot sole. This creates even more resistance to tipping, due to the longer lever arm. A difference in ski width of four mm can change the edge position from directly under the boot to two mm outside the boot sole. Think about an ice skate or in-line skate. They are both very easy to tip because the blade is narrow and lies directly under the foot. Now imagine this exaggerated situation: if the skate blade were as wide as the shoe part of the skate, it would be almost impossible to tip over. On a wide-waisted ski, the skier's knees align on the ski surface, rather than to the inside of it. This makes it much easier to keep the ski flat on the snow. Wide-waisted shaped skis have waist widths of approximately 68 to 74 mm.

Waist width and turn radius

Does the waist width of a shaped ski determine its turn radius? Will you be forced into one size of turn simply because of your alignment? Waist width is only one design characteristic of a ski. Turn radius depends on other factors, including tip and tail width, ski length, and longitudinal and torsional flex patterns. However, the waist width is a reliable guideline to determine alignment suitability, and it's easy to measure and compare when you're trying or buying skis.

The turn radii of narrow-waisted shaped skis are generally smaller than those of the wider waisted skis, but there are exceptions in each category. Most of the narrow skis have turn radii between 9 and 18 meters. (Even 18 meters is considered to be a small arc; traditional slalom and GS skis have turn radii of 33 to 40 meters.) The narrowest waisted skis with the widest tips and tails develop the most radical carved arcs. For example, some have a waist width of 62 mm, combined with a 110 mm tip and a 100 mm tail. The large difference between tip, waist, and tail means that when this ski is tipped on edge the side cut really works. In a 183 cm length, the turn radius of this ski is 12 meters. However, if the narrow-waisted ski has moderate tip and tail widths, then the turn radius will be larger. These skis still carve aggressively but because the tip and tail are not as wide they produce a larger arc. Wide-waisted shaped skis generally have turn radii of 24 to 30 meters. Some have a 74 mm waist and a 24 meter turn radius. All of these skis perform well. The narrow skis are not confined to short turns, nor are the wider skis confined to large turns. The size of your turn depends on the amount of tipping angle and ski bend. Skiers are not completely controlled by the radius or side cut designed into the ski.

Crossover Considerations

Although you know skis can influence your alignment, some skiers already have their hearts set on a certain model that may be opposite to their alignment needs. Don't despair - you can still perform successfully with a ski that is not ideally suited to you. The best solution is to get properly aligned.

If you are bowlegged and love to ski on a wide powder ski, be aware that this may not be ideal. If you ski in powder it won't affect you as much as on harder snow. You may notice that on hard snow your knees start to get sore. The ligaments and tendons are straining to overcome the resistance to tipping. Proper alignment will balance your body mass closer to the midpoint between the edges of the skis and boots. Installing a lifter under your binding will make tipping easier. It will give you more mechanical advantage or leverage, reducing the effort needed to tip the ski on edge. (Read more about lifters in a following section.)

a   *b*

Fig. 12-20. The classic knock-kneed skier, stuck on both inside edges

If you are knock-kneed but want to ski on a narrow-waisted ski there are some applications that will work. The first recommendation is to go through a complete alignment process. A lateral boot is an absolute necessity. Avoid tall lifters or tall bindings. Use a binding that puts your boot as close to the ski surface as possible. All of these recommendations combined can make the skis perform for you.

Length

Ski length affects the turn radius of any shaped ski. Typically I skied 204 cm traditional skis. Now I ski either 183 cm skis on groomed slopes and bumps or 193 cm skis on powder and bigger, steeper mountains. My 183 cm skis have a 12 meter turn radius while my 193 cm skis have a 26 meter radius. I have tested many of the newest super carve skis that are a 143 cm length, and I found them to be tremendously stable and fun. This new category of skis carves sharp, water ski type turns. They are incredibly stable on groomed snow, at high speeds and steep slopes. The required technique is lateral tipping. They are great as a training tool for skiers who want to learn to carve.

Many skiers who were weaned on traditional equipment are reluctant to downsize on the shaped skis. They find it hard to believe that a significantly shorter ski performs well. Using a shaped ski that is too long will keep most of its performance out of your reach. The ski has to bend to make an arc; if the ski is too long it may be too stiff. Manufacturers pack a lot of performance into the design. New materials make these skis very strong and high performers in short lengths. You won't obtain the arcing ability or thrill if you oversize the shaped skis. Fifteen to twenty centimeters shorter is the average downsize.

c

Selecting Shaped Skis

Most of the major ski companies have a selection that offers wide and narrow-waisted shaped skis. Any model of shaped ski will turn more easily and carve better than traditional skis. Following the recommendations for waist width based on the alignment guidelines will make your next new ski easier and more enjoyable.

What are Lifters and Plates? Are They for Everyone?

You may have noticed skiers using extra plates or devices that lift the boots higher off the skis. These lifters can perform several functions:

1. Lift the skier higher off the ski surface
2. Dampen the vibrations in the ski
3. Allow the ski to bend independently of the binding mount
4. Increase torsional (twisting resistance) and longitudinal stiffness

Not all lifters perform all the same functions. Item (1) is achieved with every plate. Items (3) and (4) are different and have opposite design and performance results.

Let's address item (1). Adding material under the binding results in the foot being farther from the top of the ski. This added leg length increases leverage or tipping ability. Because the lever arm increases (in this case the leg is further away from the ski edge fulcrum), the amount of force required to tip the ski is reduced but the distance that the lever travels is increased. This does two things to the skier. First, it is easier to tip the ski so less resistance is felt. Second, it takes longer to get to an angle because the lever has to travel farther. Of course, if you increase the speed of the tipping action you will make up the difference in time. This may sound picky and insignificant, but the combination of ski shape, lifter, and boot type can go either way, in your favor or against it. The culmination of equipment selection should be an enhancement of your ability to move on skis, so it is important to understand these features.

If you add lifters to narrow-waisted skis, they tip even more easily. We know from the earlier section about skis and alignment that knock-kneed skiers already tip too easily and too far. From that information we draw the conclusion that knock-kneed skiers benefit from wider skis without lifters. They should be as close to the ski as possible to minimize alignment shimming. On the other hand, the bowlegged skier benefits from the lifter and narrow ski combination. The bowlegged skier who wants to ski wide-waisted skis should definitely use lifters.

Another skiing benefit to come from using lifters is the increased subtlety that is gained from travel distance of the lever (the leg). Because this increases the time needed to move to the ski edge, it enables more progressive tipping movements. Tipping is one of the primary movements that is important in all facets of skiing. It is an advantage to refine this movement with equipment. Lifters can provide more gradual edge engagement and help the skier develop finesse in edging movements.

Glossary

Adduction: Movement of body extremities toward the center or middle line of the body.

Adductors: Muscles located on the inside of the femur that pull and help rotate the upper leg toward the centerline of the body.

Arc: Part of a curve, shape of a ski turn; a ski turning so that it describes this shape

Biomechanics: Study of mechanics when it is limited to living structures, i.e. the human body. Generally, biomechanics is the study of the effects that forces have upon the state of rest or motion of the human body.

Bowlegged: Stance that demonstrates knees apart or moving apart.

Carving: An arc where the ski edge is engaged and the tail follows the same line as the tip. The turn defines a clean, narrow line in the snow surface. Carving maximizes use of ski design and shape.

Cat track: Roads on the mountain that are used for service by ski area vehicles such as Sno-Cat. Cat tracks are open to skiers and usually cross and connect trails.

Christie: A skidded turn in which the skis are parallel through some part of the arc.

Co-contraction: Simultaneous muscle contraction of movers and antagonists to modify or stabilize joint activity.

Fall line: Steepest direction down the slope, where gravity has its greatest pull.

Femur rotation: Turning of the large, upper leg bone along its length, in the pelvis.

Foot inversion: Tipping the foot so that its sole faces the other foot, or faces the body centerline

Knock-kneed: Stance that demonstrates knees touching or moving together.

Kinesiology: The study of human motion.

Lateral movements: Movements from or toward the sides of the body.

Milestone: Stage of accomplishment or level of proficiency in a predetermined movement sequence.

Mud wamp: A small, Golden Retriever-sized puddle that irresistibly attracts Goldens on hot days.

Parallel match: When skis are brought to a parallel position.

Phantom Move: Activity of the free foot and ankle to invert the free foot and bring it close to the stance foot. This creates ski-turning actions.

Pre-absorbing: Flexing actions of the legs in varied terrain at higher speeds that anticipate and reduce impacts.

Primary Movements: The first and most important in an order of movements that starts at the foot; the movement from which balancing reactions in the kinetic chain originate.

Sideslipping: Moving generally sideways down the slope with skis parallel and aimed across the slope. To move in this fashion, the skis must be flattened to the snow.

Side stepping: From a standing position across the fall line, stepping sideways up or down the slope, moving one ski at a time while keeping the skis parallel.

Skeletal alignment and stacking: Alignment of the body's bones such that strength is maximized in resisting forces.

Steering and rotary movements: Traditional method of twisting parts of the body to move or stop movement of the skis. Movements initiated with leg rotation are gross motor movements that have a negative influence on precise ski control.

Ski with the Author

Here's your chance to ski with Harald Harb and his hand-selected and personally trained staff.

This is a ski experience you will never forget—it could change your skiing for life. Harald Harb and Diana Rogers are the authors and producers of the *Anyone Can Be An Expert Skier* book and video series. Their company, Harb Ski Systems, offers camps and individual lessons using the techniques described in their books and videos for skiers of all levels and abilities.

Harald invented the PMTS Direct Parallel® system, which has caught the imagination of skiers and ski instructors all over the USA. Harald is also a pioneer in the art of alignment, foot bed design, and boot fitting. All Harb Ski Systems' Green/Blue and Blue/Dark Blue camps include indoor and on-snow alignment evaluations. The All-Mountain and Race camps include an on-snow evaluation; while indoor evaluations can be scheduled individually outside of camp hours.

**For more information about the Harb Ski Systems camps—
including enrollment details, schedules, and prices—visit the Harb
Ski Systems Web site: www.harbskisystems.com or call 303-567-4663.**